Mindful Meditations

SUSAN GREGG

Penguin
Random
House

Publisher Mike Sanders
Managing Editor Jill Thomas
Acquisitions Editor Ann Barton
Senior Development Jan Lynn
Copy Editor Rick Kughen
Art Director William Thomas
Cover Designer Jessica Lee
Layout Ayanna Lacey
Indexer Brad Herriman
Proofreader Lisa Himes

First American Edition, 2022
Published in the United States by DK Publishing
6081 E. 82nd Street, Indianapolis, IN 46250

22 23 24 25 26 10 9 8 7 6 5 4 3 2 1
001-328320-MAY2022

Published in the United States by Dorling Kindersley Limited.

Library of Congress Catalog Number: 2022931018
ISBN: 978-0-74405-696-9

DK books are available at special discounts when purchased
in bulk for sales promotions, premiums, fundraising,
or educational use. For details, contact:
SpecialSales@dk.com

Printed and bound in the USA

For the curious
www.dk.com

Contents

Introduction

You hold in your hands a book that can really change your life if you let it. You can learn to use mindfulness and these short, guided meditations to reduce stress, control pain, and improve the quality of your life in numerous ways. As a side, this book will help you create more joy and happiness.

Actually, you can learn to use meditation to create whatever you want. It just takes a little discipline (to use the meditations) and a bit of dedication to your own happiness. Meditation is such a powerful tool, though we often make it harder than it needs to be.

I've taught meditation for well over 30 years. One of the first questions I get is, "How do I quiet my mind?" Your mind talks. That's what it does until we train it to be mindful and be a tool instead of a harsh taskmaster. As the title implies, these meditations provide an opportunity to be more mindful and to tune in to your inherent inner wisdom. As you learn to be more mindful, you will get in touch with your truly limitless nature.

These short, guided meditations are very easy to use, though they are incredibly powerful. Your mind is a wonderfully creative bio-computer that has run amuck. I don't know about you, but I never received the operating manual for my brain (or life, for that matter).

Your mind makes a great tool once you know how to use it. You can use your mind to go on vacation without leaving home, you can feel loved and accepted amid judgment, and you can experience ease in a world that often seems very stressful.

As you learn how to use your mind effectively rather than letting your old, limiting thoughts run the show, it is amazing how easily you can transform your life. The short, guided meditations in this book will show you how to get rid of stress, be happy no matter what, relax, walk on the beach while sitting at home, and generally improve the quality of your life. Seem a bit outrageous? Believe me, it isn't!

How to Use This Book

Everyone can visualize—that's how we think. If I say, "Think about a red fire truck," you may not actually see one, but you can describe it. Some people visualize by using words, others hear sounds, and some people see detailed pictures. How you visualize is how you visualize. There is no right or wrong way to do it.

The mindful, guided meditations in this book will allow you to use your imagination to change anything. I suggest that you thoroughly read Part 1 so you understand how to use the meditations. The rest is up to you. You could start at the beginning and go through the book systematically, open the book randomly, or even look in the index and find a meditation specifically designed to cure what ails you.

Just relax, have fun, and allow for the possibility that this stuff can work for you, too. When I was first introduced to this type of meditation, I thought it might work for other people, but it certainly wouldn't work for me.

Over the past 40 years, I have witnessed amazing results in people's lives if they were willing to use the meditations. So, be ready to let go of some of your old beliefs and, as we say here in Hawaii, "Tie your slippers tight because you're in for quite a ride."

This book is divided into four parts:

Part 1: Mindfulness, Meditation, and Your Brain

This part shows you how to use short meditations and explains a bit about how your brain operates.

Part 2: Being Present for Your Life

This part explores how you can improve the quality of your life in any area you'd like to change. Different thoughts and different beliefs result in different outcomes.

Part 3: How Else Can I Do That?

This part is full of new ways you can look at life, while showing you how to get in touch with the limitless possibilities your life holds.

Part 4: So, Now What?

This part includes numerous ways to use mindfulness. You'll find short, guided meditations to apply the techniques you've learned.

Extras

I love quotes, so you'll find quotes scattered throughout this book. They might help you think differently, and perhaps they will even guide and inspire you.

Acknowledgments

The list of people I would like to thanks is endless. So many wonderful people have touched my life.

First, I would like to thank you, the reader, for choosing to read this book. I hope you apply what you'll learn in your daily life. Change occurs in the moment, and you can build on that moment by consciously choosing to think differently.

I would also like to thank my father for believing in me when no one else did and my mom for her love of the written word.

I am very grateful The Beatles found Maharishi Mahesh Yogi and introduced me and the world to Transcendental Meditation.

I have had many wonderful teachers, starting with Jean Lang, an incredibly gentle, loving soul. Don Miguel Ruiz and Sister Sarita, you have my eternal gratitude and love. I am so glad I had the opportunity to spend all those years with you before the rest of the world found you when you released The Four Agreements.

What an incredible gift this journey called life has been. I feel so blessed. There is no way I can fully express my love and gratitude to my partner Bea and the rest of the fur family. Muffy, although you are long gone, you are always in my heart.

Finally, I want to thank the universe for rainbows.

Trademarks

Part 1

Mindfulness, Meditation, and Your Brain

Your brain is an incredible biocomputer, but most of us never received the instruction manual, or if we did, we didn't read it.

You can do just about anything with your mind once you know how. I still remember how frustrated I used to get trying to use my first computer in the early 1980s. If you've never used a computer, even though it is capable of doing lots of wonderful things, you may find it hard to get it to do even the simplest tasks. The same is true of your brain.

You know how to think, but how focused or mindful are you about what you focus your attention on? Your habitual thinking will just create more of the same old, same old.

You want to be happy, yet unconsciously your thoughts create stress and disharmony. You can learn to use your mind to create what you want, when you want, and you don't have to leave the comfort of your favorite chair to do it.

These guided meditations will help you retrain your mind. The concepts in these meditations will help you focus your attention on what you do want.

Chapter 1

Mindfulness, Meditations, and Happiness

Imagine you just bought the most amazing car. It automatically takes you anyplace. You tell it where you want to go, and it finds the best route while avoiding traffic jams. It can even take you to the best restaurants and make reservations for you. It would order for you if you let it. You thoroughly enjoy sitting back and letting your car drive you wherever you want to go. It even finds the perfect parking space and then parks for you.

Then one day, you're on your way to the movies, and you see your best friend stranded by the side of the road. It is pouring out, and she frantically tries to wave you down. You tell the car to stop, but it won't. It has begun to think it is in charge. It believes it doesn't need to listen to you anymore; it's the boss and knows better.

Your brain is a lot like that car. You may have forgotten that your brain is your tool. Your mind tells you the same stories, and you have allowed it to wander, believe its version of reality while creating the same emotions and habitual responses.

As long as your mind is in charge, making a change of any kind becomes a real struggle. Your mind takes you wherever it habitually wants to go. It talks endlessly, and you allow its opinions to dictate your emotional response to life. Once you retrain your mind, you can use it consciously to create what you *do* want. Instead of creating stress, you can train your mind to see life in a limitless manner. You can focus on feeling loved and begin to make all your choices from a place of love instead of fear.

As you begin to use your brain as a tool instead of allowing it to be a relentless taskmaster, your experience changes dramatically, you feel better, life becomes easier, and you'll be much happier.

The Amazing Brain

Your brain is a virtual chemical factory continuously manufacturing a whole range of opiate-like substances that can create anything from pure bliss and euphoria to mild stress or severe depression. It's time for you to learn how to retrain your brain so you can choose how you want to feel.

Imagine yourself holding a juicy lemon in your hand. Feel its waxy skin. Look at it closely. Notice the texture, the way it feels in your hand, its weight, and how it smells. As you think of the smell, you cut the lemon in half, feeling the juices as they flow over your hand. Now, mentally pick the lemon up and take a big bite. As you mentally bite into that lemon, your mouth may salivate as you imagine biting into that lemon. Your mind doesn't know the difference between a memory and an actual event. You do, but your biocomputer doesn't.

If I gave you directions to relax deeply, put you into an altered state of consciousness, and gave you a suggestion to experience something, your mind would gladly go along with the suggestion. An altered state of consciousness is simply a state of awareness that's different, more relaxed than normal everyday awareness. If you were relaxed enough, I could touch your arm with an ice cube, tell you it was a hot iron, and your body would immediately create a blister. Your mind controls all your movements, maintains your body's temperature, controls the digestion of food, and takes care of hundreds of details without you having to do anything consciously.

Your mind automatically filters out hundreds of pieces of information, tells you what you are feeling, and stores tons of data. Hopefully, right now, your mind is helping you stay focused on what you are reading. Or your mind could tell you that what you are reading is boring, useless, and it could be distracting you, wandering, or worrying about something totally unrelated. You may not be aware of the people around you, the colors of the objects in your environment, or notice all the different sounds and smells. If you were aware of all the details, your ability to focus would be minimal.

You can learn to use your mind's inherent abilities to vastly improve the quality of your life. You already have the tool; it's just a matter of learning how to use it. Your mind, your body, and your experience of life are all linked. You already know how to create stress. With the aid of the meditations in this book, you will learn to be more mindful about what you consciously focus your attention on and do it more mindfully. You can create ease or stress, happiness or misery, or almost anything else you want from life.

How the Brain Works

Brain research is still in its infancy. Yet, each day, researchers learn more about how the brain operates and realize there is still so much more to learn. Your mind produces brain waves in the form of electromagnetic waves, neuropeptides, hormones, and a variety of other chemicals.

Neuropeptides have been referred to as the molecules of emotions, and your brain produces over 100 different kinds. These neuropeptides help your brain communicate with your body. All your cells have receptors and utilize or "eat" the peptides your brain excretes. So, if you are angry often, your cells become habituated to "angry" peptides. If you use mental imagery to create bliss, happiness, and joy, your cells will develop an appetite for them, and your brain will produce more of them.

Life does not consist mainly, or even largely, of facts and happenings. It consists mainly of the storm of thoughts that is forever flowing in one's head.

—Mark Twain, writer and humorist

Even though we can't fully understand how our brains work, we can utilize what we do know. Because our minds don't know the difference between what we are experiencing externally and what we are imagining internally, we can use guided meditations to "trick" our brains into feeling differently.

Your imagination is just as real to your brain as life itself. Many doctors believe that up to 80 percent of all illnesses are stress-induced. Your body responds to stress physically, yet stress isn't created by life. Stress is created by the chemical factory in your brain. One person may find something stressful while another person finds the same thing relaxing. Stress is created by what you tell yourself about life. So, you can also use your mind to reduce the effect of stress and relieve the symptoms.

Brain Facts

Brain scans have found that the same portions of the brain are activated by the memory of an experience and the experience itself. Numerous studies show guided meditations can change your brain chemistry, which in turn, affects your overall health.

Here are some other facts about your brain:

- Your brain can produce a variety of different electromagnetic brain waves. Just like shifting gears in a car, your brain shifts gears when you are thinking, sleeping, or meditating.
- Gamma waves are involved in problem solving and perception and are present when you are afraid. Their frequency range is approximately 26 to 80 Hz (transitions or cycles per second).
- Beta waves are associated with waking consciousness. Beta waves are activity above 12 Hz.
- Alpha waves are electromagnetic oscillations in the frequency range of 8 to 12 Hz. These waves are often associated with meditation and other forms of relaxation like yoga.
- Theta rhythms are waveforms associated with various sleep states, deep relaxation, and meditative states. They are between 4 and 8 Hz and are often accessed during guided meditations.
- Delta waves are large, slow (2 Hz or less) brain waves associated with deep sleep.

What Are Guided Meditations?

I think of guided meditations as a fun game of mindfully focusing our thoughts. They are a wonderful opportunity to "let's play pretend": I say imagine yourself standing next to a beautiful waterfall, and you pretend to be standing next to a waterfall.

In Chapter 2, I will explain the nuts and bolts of how to participate in guided meditations, but for now, let's just talk about what you can do with them and what they can do for you.

As I've said, our brains really don't know the difference between a memory, an image we've created mentally, and an event happening right here, right now. Therefore, we can use our minds to make profound changes using mental imagery.

With mindfulness and/or a guided meditation, you can:

- Dramatically reduce stress levels.
- Feel as if you've taken a vacation without ever leaving home.
- Sleep better.
- Experience more intimacy and get along better with the people in your life.
- Get rid of destructive habits and behaviors.
- Improve your ability to concentrate.
- Get rid of phobias and fears.
- Enhance your ability to love and accept yourself.
- Be happier and just generally improve the quality of your life.
- Modify your health and change your body.
- Relieve chronic pain.

A guided meditation is a form of visualization. In a guided meditation, you use your mind to visualize images that help you relax and assist you in retraining your mind.

The list can go on and on. Basically, you can use guided meditations to do whatever you want. Later in the book, I'll even show you how to create your own visualizations. What you do with your mind is limited only by your willingness to play, the depth of your decision to let go of limiting beliefs, and your commitment to yourself.

If you put an ice cube in a cup of hot tea, it has no choice but to melt. These meditations are designed to help you find the peace and joy that lives deep within your being. So, relax and allow the words to work their magic in your life!

Do I Really Have to Quack Like a Duck?

Most often, when people hear the word hypnosis, they often think about people running around onstage making fools of themselves or someone quitting smoking or losing weight. Hypnosis is one of many ways to get into an altered state. When you go into an altered state, you are more relaxed, your mind is more suggestible, so it is more open to learning and accepting of change.

Milton Erickson was a well-known physician who used a combination of hypnosis and teaching stories in his work. For centuries, spiritual teachers have used teaching stories to convey their messages. Dr. Erickson was able to use this combination to get phenomenal results. At the time of his death, he had a one-year waiting list for a consultation.

People continue to study his work. He would sit with a person, tell him a story, and his life would change dramatically. The meditations in this book work at many different levels. They are a form of teaching stories as well as meditations.

There are only two ways to live your life.
One is as though nothing is a miracle. The other is
as though everything is.

—Albert Einstein, physicist

Seeing Is Believing

Images are in the eye—well, actually, they are in the mind—of the beholder. Each of your eyes "sees" an image, and then the brain puts them together into a three-dimensional object. If you've ever reached for something under a few feet of water, then you realize how easily your mind can be deceived. Your mind tells you the object is in one place while your hand and eyes realize it is several inches away.

When shown photographs by anthropologists, aborigine tribes that have never seen photographs had to learn to "see" the picture before they could see the image in the photograph. When they first looked at a photo, they only saw a series of dots. Their minds had to learn how to put the dots together so they could finally see the image.

For a while, 3D pictures were very popular. On the surface, you would see geometric designs, but if you changed your focus, you could see three-dimensional pictures pop right out of the designs. Of course, if you didn't believe the pictures were there and you never looked for them, you wouldn't be able to see them.

So, I suggest that for a time, you suspend any judgments or disbeliefs. Join me in a game of "let's play pretend" and see what happens.

Take a long, slow, and deep breath. Really expand your chest and your stomach. Just focus your attention on feeling your breath. Where do you feel it? Perhaps in your nose, the back of your mouth, your chest, or your stomach? Just take another long, slow, deep breath and notice. When you think your lungs are full, breathe in a little more air.

Now, as you breathe out, imagine yourself breathing out any judgments, cares, concerns, or stress that you have. Just blow it all out like you are blowing out a candle, and mentally let go. When you inhale, imagine yourself breathing in a feeling of peace and relaxation. Do that for a few moments and notice how you feel.

Remember, this is simply a pretend game, so no matter what thoughts your mind shares, just focus your attention on your breathing and notice how you feel. Your breath is a very powerful tool once you begin to use it consciously. I'll tell you more about how to use your breath in Chapter 2.

> Life is a magic vase filled to the brim; so made that you cannot dip into it nor draw from it; but it overflows into the hand that drops treasures into it–drop in malice and it overflows hate; drop in charity and it overflows love.
>
> —John Ruskin, social critic and author

Work That Muscle We Call the Mind!

If you join the gym and never go, your body probably won't change much. If you go to the gym regularly but never lift any weights, there still won't be much change. But if you go to the gym regularly and work out vigorously, your body will change. If you hire a personal trainer to push you to do more and help you meet your goals, and then if you follow their suggestions, you will progress even faster. With their help, you can create the body of your dreams.

You can think of this book as your membership to the universal gym of personal growth, love, happiness, joy, and ease. If you use the meditations regularly, your life will change. Think of me as your personal coach and follow the suggestions throughout the book so you can create the life of your dreams. Actually, my experience has been that you will create a life beyond your wildest dreams.

The more you practice, the greater the benefits and the easier it will be. Once you learn how to ride a bike, you never forget. Learning to ride the bike does take practice. Using guided meditations also takes a little bit of practice, but the benefits are well worth the effort.

Quieting your mind is not about not thinking. It is about learning to be more mindful in the moment. If I say to you, "Whatever you do, do not think about a red fire truck," you immediately think about a red fire truck.

Mindfulness is about learning how to focus your mind differently. A wonderful way to be more mindful and quiet your mind is to imagine yourself standing in a train station. Trains constantly come and go. You can get on one, go for a ride, and get off whenever you want. Imagine your thoughts as trains. They come, and they go. You can go for a ride or just stand on the platform and watch it go by. As soon as you notice you have gone for a ride, you can get off at the next station. Just watch your thoughts. If you notice you've been thinking instead of observing, just change that thought.

In this chapter, you have begun to understand that your mind is an amazing tool but a terrible master. You can expand your awareness, change your thinking and in the process, change your life dramatically. You are also beginning to realize that your brain is an incredible bio-computer. You're beginning to understand that your mind is a machine that uses waves and manufactures chemicals to "create'" your experience of life. Your experience of life is based on the stories your mind tells you and not life itself.

In the next chapter, we explore a variety of ways for you to relax into the meditations.

Chapter 2

Going Deeper and Deeper

To someone terrified of snakes, a picture of a snake crawling all over another person can be just as disturbing as the snake itself. Mental imagery is incredibly powerful, and you can easily learn to harness it. Whatever you consistently focus your attention on, you get more of. If you allow your habitual thought patterns to run rampant, you will continue to have the same experiences in your life. You will get the same results unless and until you change your thoughts. Your thoughts do become things in your life. If stress is a regular part of your life, you will create more stress. If peace of mind eludes you, it will remain elusive until you make some internal changes.

The nice part is that you can use your mind's ability to relax to create more of what you do want. You can use these meditations to relieve stress or create stress. It all depends on your inner dialogue. You already know how to visualize, and you can create stress or ease depending on how you focus your awareness. You don't necessarily do it consciously, but you do create it with your mental images.

You already have all the necessary skills. The meditations in this book will show you how to consciously use those skills in a more positive, life-enhancing way. By mindfully focusing your attention on what you do want instead of worrying about what you don't want, your life will change dramatically.

You can do this. Anyone can. You just need to apply a bit of patience, practice, some determination, and a little bit of discipline.

I used to hate the two D's—discipline and dedication. I avoided them at all costs until I realized what powerful, transformational tools they are.

Happiness is an internal choice, moment by moment, thought by thought. Happiness isn't dependent on having more money, or time or a romantic partner. Happiness is a choice and is totally independent of external events.

When Emotions Are in Charge

Your brain produces waves and chemicals. It also produces a variety of levels of consciousness. Psychobiologists—scientists who explore the relationship between the brain, emotions, and other biological processes—have discovered fascinating things about the brain's three levels of consciousness and the role of the limbic brain in your thought process.

Your brain is like a trinity. There is your reptilian brain, which controls things like breathing, heartbeat, and swallowing. Next, there is your limbic brain, where your emotions are stored. Finally, there is the neocortical brain, where speaking, planning, and reasoning reside.

It's your limbic brain that really gets things cooking. Your mind doesn't really deal with facts. It deals with an emotional interpretation of the facts. Once you realize that, you can use your emotional reactions to your benefit. The stronger the emotions are, the stronger your reaction will be. It is important to realize that all your emotions are generated by the stories you tell yourself about events in your life and not the events themselves.

An automobile engine has a transmission that shifts gears so the engine can be more efficient. You can learn to shift gears emotionally so you can create more of what you want in your life. You can use your emotions rather than be used by them.

I still remember the day my mom was trying to teach me how to drive. She had me stop the car in the middle of a very steep hill. I was just learning to drive a stick shift and thought I would never get that car going. I'd pop the clutch, and the car would stall. She made me try repeatedly. I got out of the car dramatically, screamed, and yelled. She just sat there and waited until I was finally able to get the car moving again. I finally made it up the hill. She had me stop and try to get started repeatedly. Eventually, I learned to shift gears effortlessly and start and stop on any hill. Had she not done that, I may never have learned.

With a bit of practice, you can learn to shift your emotional gears, too. What amazing freedom that ability brings into your life! As you learn to choose your emotions, your ability to make choices is so much easier, and what you choose becomes clearer.

You no longer need to feel like a victim to life. As you become more familiar with mindfulness and practice using the short meditations in this book, you'll find happiness and ease are always just a thought away.

Shifting Gears

This meditation shows you how to play with your emotions and literally change how you are feeling, at will.

Think about something that brings you a feeling of joy. It could be a sunrise, a sunset, a puppy or a kitten, your best friend, a baby, or your beloved. Breathe in that feeling of joy. Really focus on how it feels in your body. Is your chest relaxed? Does your heart feel open? Is your stomach full or empty or full of butterflies? How does your stomach feel?

Take a few long, slow, deep breaths while consciously letting go of that feeling. As you breathe, imagine letting go of that expansive feeling of love. See the feeling just falling away.

Now think about something you find upsetting. It could be a noisy neighbor, being stuck in a traffic jam, getting hollered at by your boss, or having a huge fight with a family member. Focus on how the upset feels in your body. Are your chest and stomach tight or relaxed? Is your heart closed? How does it feel in your body?

Fully let go of that feeling. Just imagine shaking it off and letting it go.

Now think about the thing that brings you the feeling of joy. Once again, focus on the feeling of joy. Where do you feel joy in your body? If your heart feels open, take a few long, deep breaths and expand that feeling in your chest. Focus on the feeling of joy and make it bigger.

Now think about something you find upsetting again. Expand that feeling. Now focus on the feeling of joy. Practice shifting gears for a few minutes, and simply go back and forth between the two emotions.

Allow it to be fun, easy, and effortless. Just like a pendulum swinging back and forth, switch emotional gears.

It may take a bit of practice, but it will make a huge difference in your life once you master this skill.

Finding Out What Works for You

Using the short meditations in this book is easy, but your mind can make it very complicated if you listen to it. Guided meditations are simple and very effective. All you must do is breathe deeply, relax, and play along with the words. Just practice using your imagination to experience the images. You read a meditation and allow yourself to visualize the words.

As you read the meditations in this book, take a few minutes for yourself. Before you start a meditation, take a few long, deep breaths and give yourself permission to relax. You can set the stage, signaling it's time to meditate. Perhaps light a scented candle, sit in a comfortable chair, and then randomly open the book or find a meditation that speaks directly to what is going on in your life. Breathe deeply and then slowly read one of the meditations and allow it to guide you and open your heart and really feel it. You can play with the images randomly throughout the day. Make them yours. Change them, personalize them, and above all else, *play* with them and let them play with you.

Later in this chapter, you will find a variety of ways to relax and get ready for the meditations, called *inductions*. Inductions refer to the beginning of a guided meditation, where you are led through a process that will help you relax. Inductions open your heart and your mind, so you are more receptive to the suggestions in the meditation. You can use them alone without a meditation to just relax. You can record the meditations on your phone, so you can listen to them whenever you want. There are many ways to use them. After all, life is full of limitless possibilities unless you decide to limit yourself.

Mastering your mind takes practice, and it will make a huge difference in your life. Occasionally, I will remind you to relax before a meditation. You can use one of the inductions in this chapter to make up your own meditation, or you can just remember to breathe and relax.

The Rose

Everyone knows how to visualize, but we all do it differently. While one person may see images, another person may feel or hear them. This meditation helps you practice visualization. If you try hard, images often remain elusive, so just allow yourself to relax and, above all else, have fun.

Think about a beautiful rose. What color is it? (You get to choose your favorite color). Make it vivid.

Imagine a single drop of dew on the edge of one of the petals. Allow yourself to be with the image quietly. How do you perceive it? If you find yourself saying, "I can't see a rose," just let go of that thought and think about a rose. What color is it? How big is it? Does it have a scent? Can you see any thorns? Just allow yourself to play with the idea of a rose.

Focus on the texture of the petals. Is the rose fully open or is it a bud? Imagine yourself getting really tiny and sliding down the petal of the rose. When you reach the end of the petal, see yourself floating effortlessly in the air.

Is the rose alone, in a garden, or in part of a beautiful bouquet? What does the light feel like as it reflects off your rose? What thoughts and feelings come to mind as you think about your rose?

I can guarantee that if you allow yourself to play with the image, you will be able to "see" it. We each "see" differently. Some people see visually, others "hear" the vision, and some "feel" the image. There is no right or wrong. Practice will make it easier.

Relax, breathe, and play. Those are three wonderful concepts that can add immensely to the quality of your life.

Some Thoughts on Meditation and Mindfulness

There are as many ways to meditate as there are people who do it. I have taught people how to meditate for over 40 years. The one thing I have consistently observed is that people make meditation and mindfulness much harder than it really is. Meditation can be as simple as taking a long, slow, deep breath!

Meditation is the practice of focusing the mind, and it encompasses a wide variety of spiritual practices. Meditation can be used for personal development, to achieve peace, to improve your health, and to generally enhance the quality of your life. You can do moving meditations, seated meditations, and open-eye meditations. The variations are endless.

Mindfulness

Mindfulness is very similar to meditation. It is focused awareness—being aware of what you are focusing your attention on, and consciously choosing what you are thinking about and how you are focusing.

Mindfulness can take many forms, including walking meditations. I have a labyrinth on my property and have built many of them all over the world. Slowly walking a labyrinth can be a wonderful mindful meditation. You can choose two words like "love" and "peace." When you step with one foot, you say "love," and when you step with the other foot, you say or think the word "peace."

Forest bathing is another wonderful physically-based mindfulness practice. It is a way of immersing yourself in your physical senses and slowing your mind. You walk in the forest, focusing your attention on the sights, sounds, and smells. As soon as you do, you will feel your body relax, and your mind get quieter. In Chapter 4, you will find a guided meditation on forest bathing.

Visualizations, mindfulness, or guided meditations work at many levels. They really work. If your mind says you can't do these meditations, thank it for sharing and do them anyway. Be playful and allow yourself to have fun. You can allow the time you spend with these meditations to make a difference in your life or not. It is really up to you.

You are constantly changing. You aren't even the same person who started reading this book. What you have read has already changed you. Your body automatically breathes. It is just part of what it does. Your mind thinks, and you can use what you think and how you think about it to change your experience of life in a profound way.

In five years, you will be five years older. If you never read any of these meditations and don't make any new choices, your life will be pretty much the same. If you spend a few minutes every day with these meditations and apply some of the things you are learning, your life will change dramatically. Fast-forward five years—which choice do you wish you had made? So, make it now. Make the choice to spend a few minutes on yourself each day—and then do it!

So, just breathe and read on. In a moment, I will introduce you to a variety of ways to relax and get centered. They will make working with the meditations easier and more effective. These inductions are a simple way to shift gears mentally. To get the most out of the meditations, it helps if your brain is producing mostly alpha waves. So, these inductions will help you relax, which in turn will invite your brain to slow down and slip into alpha.

I suggest you try them all. Each time you read a meditation, use a different one until you find which ones are most effective for you. One day, one will work great, while another day, it won't. So, remain flexible and use whatever works best on any given day. Remember, the only way this stuff won't work for you is if you don't use it. Just using the inductions alone can help you relax and reduce stress.

You might want to keep a journal or make notes in the margin of the book. One of my only regrets is that I didn't journal about my journey with meditations and mindfulness.

Relaxing

As you read these inductions out loud or to yourself, read the words slowly and mindfully. Give yourself the opportunity to really feel, see, and experience them. Stretch out each word and allow your thoughts to be soft and gentle. Pause often as you read, take a deep breath before you continue, and allow the ideas to settle in. Let the words impact you. Speak and think very, very slowly.

I find it helps to imagine long pauses between the words. I see my thoughts spaced further and further apart. It helps me relax and slows down my thoughts.

Breathe Deep and Know

Your breath is one of the most powerful tools for change that you have. You can use it in many ways. You can use it to relax, let go of limiting beliefs, or energize your body. You will learn many ways to use it throughout the book. Here you use your breath to relax and connect to the essence of who and what you really are.

Focus your attention on your breathing. Take a long, slow, deep breath and notice where you feel it in your body. Do you feel it in your throat? In your chest? Your nose? Your stomach? Where exactly do you feel your breath?

Now, take another long, slow, deep breath and mentally give yourself permission to relax. As you breathe in, breathe in relaxation, and as you breathe out, breathe out anything that is unlike relaxation. Slowly settle down into yourself like a leaf gently floating in the wind.

Slowly focus your attention on your breath and let go. Deep within you lies a place that is always at peace, always at ease. Allow yourself to connect with it now. Slowly breathe in peace and breathe out anything that is unlike peace. Focus on your breathing and allow yourself to go deeper and deeper within yourself. Breathe and allow yourself to connect with that place of peace. Focus slowly and gently on your breath. Feel it as it moves in and out of your body. With each breath, allow yourself to become more relaxed, more at peace, and more at ease.

A good rule for mental conduct—think whatever it makes you truly happy to think.

—Black Elk, holy man of the Oglala Sioux

Stairway to Peace

This is a fun visualization. You can make the stairs as steep or as gradual as you like. Imagine they are indoors or out in nature. Make them as grand or as humble as you'd like.

Imagine yourself at the top of a long staircase. The stairs are beautiful, and as you slowly begin to walk down, you feel a sense of peace, joy, and ease. Slowly, step by step, you go deeper and deeper. You find yourself becoming more and more relaxed with each step you take.

As you walk down the staircase, you notice the stairs are changing texture and form. They are becoming softer. The light beckons you. Slowly, step by step, you find yourself relaxing totally and completely. You let go of any cares and concerns and allow yourself to relax.

You breathe deeply and enjoy the process of walking down farther and farther, deeper and deeper. With each step you take, you become fully relaxed, at peace, and at ease. The light takes on a golden glow that fills you with a sense of connection, peace, and ease. By the time you reach the last step, you are completely and totally relaxed.

Ten, Nine, Eight ...

Counting backward is another wonderful way to relax. You can also use this induction if you are having difficulty falling asleep.

Imagine the number 10. See it flashing and glowing, like a huge, multicolored billboard. See the number 10 getting bigger and bigger and then imagine it floating effortlessly away like it has a large balloon attached to it.

Now see the number 9. See it getting bigger and bigger, twirling effortlessly as it floats away, taking all your cares and concerns with it. As the number 9 drifts away, you find yourself more relaxed and at ease.

By the time you reach the number 1, you will be totally and completely relaxed, at peace, and at ease.

Now see the number 8 come into your line of sight and then float away. See the number 7 and the number 6 linked together and slowly floating upward and lazily drifting away from you. You breathe deeply and feel yourself relax as you watch the numbers get smaller and smaller.

The number 5 slowly comes into view. It is colorful and peaceful to look at. You watch it as it gently floats, twirling as it goes higher and higher, and you become more and more relaxed. By the time you see the number 1, you will be totally relaxed.

Now watch numbers 4, 3, and 2 come into view. Imagine a string attached to them, and as they float away, all your cares and concerns float away with them. Now you see a great big 1, and you take a deep breath and totally let go.

Learning how to release stress improves the quality of your life, and it can save your life!

Stress affects your thinking, behavior, and mood. You may

- Become irritable and intolerant of even minor disturbances.
- Feel jumpy or exhausted all the time.
- Find it hard to concentrate.
- Worry about insignificant things.
- Doubt your abilities.
- Feel frustrated, lose your temper, and yell at others for no apparent reason.
- Imagine negative, terrifying scenes.
- Feel you have missed opportunities.

Slowing Down

When we are stressed, we tend to think in circles, and our thoughts come in rapid succession. This induction is a wonderful way to slow down, smooth out the wrinkles in your thinking, and feel more relaxed.

Take a long, slow, deep breath. Focus your attention on your breathing and consciously make it slower and slower. When you have inhaled as deeply as you can, stop your breath for a moment and then slowly exhale. When you are done exhaling again, pause your breath before you slowly inhale again.

Next, focus your attention on your thoughts. Observe them as they go by. Imagine you are standing at a train station, and your thoughts are like trains coming in and out of the station. Imagine your thoughts as they slow down and come to a stop. When a thought comes to mind, just slow the words down until there is a space between each one. Gently expand the space between them until your thoughts are just barely moving.

Focus your attention on your breathing again. Allow your chest and stomach to relax as you continue to breathe slowly and deeply. Completely fill your chest and then let go. As you exhale completely, empty your torso and let go.

Gently and totally allow yourself to relax.

Shushing Down the Slide

This is a fun way to imagine relaxing.

Imagine you are at the top of a huge water slide. The water is at a perfect temperature, and you feel totally safe and protected. It is a lot like floating in the womb. You start to slide down. You go down and down. You lie back and enjoy the feeling. The water gently rocks you back and forth. You feel more and more relaxed.

Allow yourself to be in the flow of the water slide. Imagine yourself gently shushing down the flume, feeling alive, relaxed, and nurtured by the experience. The farther down you go, the more relaxed you are. The sound of the water rushing by is very peaceful.

You look up and watch the clouds as you continue to float effortlessly along. You take a long, slow, deep breath and let go, relax, and feel at peace. The water washes away any cares or concerns and leaves you feeling relaxed and refreshed, open, and willing to let go of anything that holds you back.

In the Arms of the Beloved

One of the most valuable questions I ever answered for myself was, "Is this a safe universe or a hostile one?" For a long time, I viewed it as a hostile one, but once I began connecting with my spiritual self, I realized it was a very safe universe. I don't really see the universe as an entity, but for this induction, I suggest you imagine that the universe can embrace you and that its embrace is safe, loving, and nurturing.

Imagine yourself being enfolded in the loving arms of the universe. Feel the gentle, loving touch. Allow yourself to lean back into that embrace and feel the sense of peace, love, and unconditional acceptance that fills you.

Surrender to that love. Let go of anything that is unlike peace and acceptance. Feel the wind come up and blow away anything that no longer serves you. You effortlessly let go of any resistance or emotions that rise to the surface. You allow yourself to be embraced, loved, and healed by the beloved.

Only put off until tomorrow what you are willing to die having left undone.

—Pablo Picasso, artist

Wide Awake, Feeling Fine

One of the comments I often get is, "I relaxed like you said, and then I fell asleep." If you are very tired, you may take a short nap. If you do, you will feel very rested afterward. When you finish a meditation and are ready to return to normal, waking consciousness, I recommend you give yourself a gentle, loving suggestion. Say something like, "In a moment, I will be wide awake, feeling fine, and in perfect health. I will feel rested, relaxed, and fully awake."

If you use the meditations just before you go to sleep, give yourself a suggestion that after the meditation, you will easily fall asleep, have a wonderful night's rest, and wake in the morning fully energized.

Take a few minutes for yourself after each meditation. Allow yourself to slowly get back into your day. If you can't take some time, that's okay, too. But ideally, give yourself some time to assimilate the experience rather than jumping back into your day.

In this chapter, you learned how to use inductions to relax and change the way you think. You now know your thoughts become things and that if you change your thinking, your life will change. You're beginning to understand how your brain operates and how you can use it as an amazing tool instead of being used by it!

Part 2

Being Present for Your Life

We can only fully live life in the moment. When we are fully focused on the moment we can consciously create what we want. If we are worried about the future or thinking about the past, there is no room left for us in the present moment. Our thinking crowds out what is happening in the moment and we don't get to experience life. Instead of living, we think about living. When we fully savor life, we can find joy in the smallest things. We are also much more likely to make choices that will create a full and rich life.

Because life is made up of lots of ordinary moments, what if you could make the ordinary extraordinary? What if you could rejoice at being stuck in traffic, look forward to going to work, or even enjoy cleaning the house?

Believe it or not, you don't have to change "out there" in order to enjoy life. All you must do is change the way you think about the little things. Perceiving the everyday events in life in a new and more expansive way is only a breath away. So, take a deep breath and read on.

Chapter 3

Making the Mundane Magical

Life is a series of events. There is a well-known Zen saying about enlightenment: Before enlightenment, there is chopping wood and carrying water, and after enlightenment, there is chopping wood and carrying water. The main difference between before and after is your ability to be in the present moment and enjoy the process. Your inner dialogue can bring great joy or misery depending on what you believe and what perspective you energize.

We are born, we live, and then we die. Death is part of life. We get to choose how much we enjoy the time between our birth and our death. The events don't matter as much as what we tell ourselves about what happens. There is a great deal of freedom in the knowledge that we don't have to change life in order to be happy. We can learn to be happy no matter what is happening around us. Then we can fill our life with whatever we want!

The more we consciously choose what we focus our attention on, the more magical life becomes. Love expands, and fear contracts.

You can feel good about what you are doing or do things in a futile attempt to feel good. A horse pulls a wagon more efficiently than it can push one.

Enjoying what you are doing is a shortcut to happiness. It's far easier than limiting what you are willing to do so you can be happy. Happiness is an inside job.

The meditations in this chapter will help you see life differently. You can learn to look forward to going to work, paying bills, or doing the dishes!

I lived in rural Vermont in the 1960s. I was from NYC and loved talking to the "old timers." One rainy day, I was talking to Roy. He was standing by the edge of the road, bringing his herd back to the barn. I said something about the rain. He paused, looked and me, and said: "If you don't like the weather, wait a minute. Best thing you can do when it's raining is just let it rain and enjoy the rain."

So, learn to take a deep breath and accept what is, then decide to embrace it and enjoy it. What is 'is' so you may as well let yourself like it. Or you will continue to make yourself miserable by judging it. Happy or miserable is a choice we can make moment by moment, no matter what is happening.

Why Should I Love Work?

Some people love their jobs, while other people hate their work and only do it to pay the bills. It isn't the activities that are the problem; it is how we choose to approach them. I have found that if I avoid doing something because I dislike it, I have denied myself an opportunity. I used to hate doing dishes. I would wait until every dish in the house was dirty before I would do them. Then the task would be so overwhelming that it would take a long time to do, and I hated every moment of it.

Like much of life, doing the dishes or not doing them wasn't the real issue. The issue was my inability to enjoy what I was doing while I was doing it. The only moment you ever have is the present moment. If you are waiting for your happiness until you finish the job, then chances are you'll seldom experience being happy. Later never gets here because by the time it arrives, it's the present moment again. So, if you want to be happy, it helps to find a way to enjoy just about anything, including going to work, getting stuck in traffic, and even doing the dishes.

The Flower of Enlightenment: Opening Your Heart

When we don't want to do something, when we judge something, or when we are just generally unhappy, judgment and fear are the underlying emotions. When our hearts are open, and we are full of love, it is much easier to savor and fully enjoy life, no matter what is happening.

Imagine a bright, shiny, golden metal disc directly over your heart. It is three-dimensional and covered with ancient symbols of peace, wisdom, and joy. It slowly begins to spin. The symbols are projected all over the walls.

As it spins more and more rapidly, it turns into a beautiful lotus flower that opens wider and wider. Its petals are a brilliant pink, and the center of the flower begins to glow. It gets brighter and brighter, twirling and pulsing.

It opens fully, and a shaft of light flows into it, filling your heart with a deep sense of peace and love, and acceptance. You can feel the warmth of the light hitting the flower and flowing effortlessly into your heart.

It feels like a giant doorway flooding your heart with love. The golden disc continues to spin, and you can smell the sweet scent of the lotus. You remember the lotus symbolizes enlightenment, and you relax back into the feeling of love.

You feel the love washing away any old hurts and illuminating your mind, heart, and spirit. You never knew love could feel so good, and you surrender completely to it.

You gently and lovingly let go of any of your limiting beliefs, agreements, and assumptions that no longer serve you. You are joyously alive, at peace, and in love.

Giving Your Hands a Bath

I used to absolutely hate doing the dishes. I'd wait until every dish in the house was dirty before I would wash them. By that point, washing the dishes was a really big job.

Then I ran across an excerpt from one of Thich Nhat Hanh's books. In it, he talked about making everyday chores a sacred act. I started giving my hands a bath instead of washing the dishes. Now I enjoy doing them.

This meditation shows you can learn to enjoy doing the dishes. You can use the same basic idea to enjoy anything.

It's as simple as taking something you love doing and incorporating it into what you hate doing. You will find that the issue isn't about what you are doing; it's what you are telling yourself about what you are doing.

Imagine a wonderful, luxurious bathtub filled with warm, pleasantly scented bubble bath. There are candles gently glowing, and your favorite music is playing in the background. You take a deep breath and feel so grateful knowing this is a time for you to relax and rejuvenate. You spend a moment just basking in the image and allowing yourself to be filled with a sense of peace and ease.

Feel yourself sinking into the tub while all your muscles relax. The water soaks away any cares and concerns, and you feel totally at peace without a care in the world. You could stay in this tub forever. It is a place of complete peace, a place that fills you with joy and washes away anything that is unlike complete bliss.

Breathe deeply and feel a sense of peace, ease, and joy filling you. As you exhale, let go of anything that is unlike peace and ease. Slowly breathe in peace, and breathe out anything that is unlike peace.

When you feel yourself totally relaxed, imagine yourself standing in front of your kitchen sink. The dishes are neatly stacked, soaking in warm water filled with lots of bubbles. As you plunge your hands into the water, that feeling of peace and ease returns. As you slowly wash the dishes one by one, your muscles relax. You thoroughly enjoy giving your hands a warm bath, and in the process, the dishes get clean.

Here are a few visualizations for other things in life:

- Vacuuming: Imagine a beautiful, well-cut lawn, acres and acres of rolling green hills—as you vacuum your rug, imagine creating that beauty in your home.
- Going to work: Imagine being of service, helping people, and feeling very good about what you are doing.
- Driving in traffic: Feel grateful for having a car and the opportunity to be in traffic and send blessings to the people around you.

See if you can create a list of all the things you hate doing in your life. How else could you think about them? How could they become something that brings you a feeling of joy instead of dread?

Enjoying the Process

The dictionary defines *process* as a natural event marked by gradual changes that lead toward a particular result. When I decided to change my life, I had very little patience with the process. After spending almost three decades working with people, the one piece of advice that applies universally is this: allow yourself to enjoy the process.

Even something as mundane as paying bills can be fun! You can get a box or basket and regularly put all your bills in it as they arrive. (You can also make a special file on your computer.) Decorate the box with copies of $100 bills. When it is time to pay the bills, spend a few minutes being grateful that you have the opportunity to pay bills. Look at each bill as a wonderful present; then write the check or transfer the money with gratitude.

No matter what you are doing, allow yourself to enjoy the process. This is the only time you will be able to read and experience this meditation for the first time. If it is your tenth time, it is the only time you can experience it for the tenth time. You are where you are.

Judging it or wishing you were someplace else won't help you get there one moment faster. And that wish will rob you of your happiness and joy.

A Ray of Sunshine

This meditation assists you in realizing each moment is an opportunity for a new beginning. You can even use it during the day to start over and remember to enjoy the process.

Imagine yourself standing in a sheltered spot watching the sunrise. The sky is a deep blue; overhead, the stars are still shining, and the horizon is just beginning to glow. As the glow at the horizon becomes brighter, the birds begin to sing, greeting the new day.

As you watch the world slowly come alive, you feel a sense of newness, aliveness, and limitless possibilities. You notice you are feeling a little bit cold just as the sun clears the horizon. The first rays of the sun warm you and enfold you with their warmth.

You shield your eyes and celebrate this day as yet unlived. The sun goes behind a cloud bank, and the landscape changes colors. You sit and silently watch the sun as it moves higher and higher. The sun plays hide and seek with fully white clouds moving lazily along. The moisture in the air causes the sun's rays to become visible.

You play with the shadows, moving in and out of the sun. As your body warms, you move into the shadows and then back into the sun when the coolness of the air once again surrounds you. The warmth of the sun feels very loving and nurturing.

You realize each day is a new beginning. Each moment and every new day is a blank page pregnant with possibilities. You can fill this day with anything you want. You can fill the day with joy and excitement or sadness and dread. As you connect with the sun, you realize you always have the power of your choice, and the choice you make is yours.

It's not the load that breaks you down; it's the way you carry it.

—Lena Horne, singer

Make It Easier

I believe life was meant to be easy and effortless and, above all else, fun. And it can be, once we learn to change our focus. If I have to do something, I can tell myself: this is either going to be hard or it's not.

Many years ago I bought an old house and began remodeling it. I started many projects but seldom finished any. When I decided to sell the house, I made a list of everything that I needed to do. Instead of the list motivating me, I'd look at it and tell myself *I'll never get it done* and I didn't.

Now when I have a big project to do, I make a master list and then break it down to small, manageable projects. I only put things I can do on a daily basis on the smaller lists. I have an agreement with myself that when I put something on my daily list, I get it done—no excuses and no putting it off. That inner dialogue makes life so much more manageable and enjoyable. Try it—you'll find the quality of your life increasing exponentially.

In this meditation, you will visualize a new way to start your day.

Imagine waking up slowly, looking forward to your day. You relax and start your morning routine by taking out a pen and paper. You take a deep breath and focus on three things that would really make a difference in your life. Small, manageable things.

Before you write anything down, ask yourself, "Am I willing to get these things done before I go to sleep tonight?" If the answer is an easy and enjoyable "YES!" you put the item on the list, knowing that in the evening you'll check your list and it will feel wonderful to check each item off.

In the evening, you see yourself looking at the list, checking off items and feeling great about having done them.

Sensing Your Senses

When I was a young girl, my mom planted some carrots in the backyard. She didn't understand why they kept dying until she looked out of the window one day and saw me pull up a bunch of them. When she asked me why, I told her I wanted to see if they were done yet. She went on to explain to me that the carrots stopped growing after I pulled them out. She told me about being patient. It took me many years to begin to practice patience in my life.

When I started on my spiritual path, I had the same impatience. When I found myself getting frustrated with my results, I remembered the carrots and allowed myself to be open to the experiences rather than trying to force them. When I feel impatient, I smell young carrots growing in the moist earth and remember to enjoy the process.

Each person has their own unique way of processing information. Even if we are all hiking up the same mountain, we each notice different things. When you are working with the meditations, avoid comparing your experience with the suggestions I make. A great chef seldom follows the recipe exactly. They add their own special ingredient.

The special ingredient in all these meditations is you. Savor the experience and know that your experience is perfect for you. Even though experiences are different for everyone, those experiences are perfect. There is no right or wrong; there just is what is.

Life is such an incredibly sensual experience. Physical reality is so rich and full of sights, sounds, and smells. The meditations in this book will have an impact on all areas of your life long after you experience them, especially the following one.

The Five Senses

This meditation is very simple, yet it can dramatically enhance your ability to experience the richness life holds. Do it a few times, and allow its magic to continue to unfold in your life.

Take a few long, slow, deep breaths and focus on relaxing. Gently close your eyes and really feel your breath. Focus your complete attention on your sense of feeling. Feel your breath, the air on your skin, the temperature of the air, your clothes against your skin. Focus on feeling. What do you feel around and within you? If you are sitting, notice where your body is touching the chair; notice the pressure and that point of contact.

Next, focus your attention on your sense of smell. Take a deep breath, sniff the air like a dog, and notice what you smell. Smell your arm and hands, and notice each and every scent around you.

Now focus your attention on your hearing. Listen to all the little noises around you. Listen to the sounds of your breathing, to your thoughts, and to your clothes as you move. Really focus your attention on all the sounds in your world. Listen closely and see if you can hear the spaces between the sounds. Listen for the silence that gives shape to the sounds.

Begin to focus on your sense of taste. What can you taste in your mouth? Breathe in through your mouth and taste the air. Roll your tongue around and taste all the subtle flavors in your mouth. Imagine biting into your favorite piece of fruit. How would that taste?

Now, just barely open your eyes and gaze softly around you. Notice all the shapes, colors, shadows, and bright places. Look at the details of everything. Bring your hand up toward your face and look at each finger, the lines on your hands, and your fingerprints.

Slowly and methodically focus on each of your five senses four more times. Allow yourself to get more in touch with your sense of smell, touch, taste, sound, and sight. Notice which ones you are most comfortable with and practice using the others.

Our life is what our thoughts make it.

—Marcus Aurelius, Roman emperor and philosopher

Checking and Unchecking Your Options

On a computer, you can install a screen saver. I leave my computer on all day; when I am not using it, the screen goes blank, and eventually, the hard drive shuts off. It doesn't sit there offering its opinions, distracting me, or telling me what to do. In this meditation, you will install the screen saver in your mind, so it can sit quietly rather than talking endlessly.

One night, when I first got a computer, I was having a hard time sleeping. I imagined myself typing, "Go to sleep" on my mental screen and then hitting Enter. When I woke up the next morning, I realized it was a very effective way to fall asleep.

Find a comfortable place to sit, relax, and enjoy.

Imagine yourself going into the Tools option of your brain. You mentally open the toolbox, and you find a list with all the possible options. All you have to do is put a little checkmark in front of the box, and your mind will follow the directions. You can also uncheck boxes if you no longer want your brain to do something.

There is a long list of options. As you scroll down the list, you notice the box marked "Judge everything" is checked, so you uncheck it. You also notice checks in front of "Fear," "Talk endlessly," "Offer my opinion on things," "Hold on to old beliefs at any cost," and "Make change hard." You uncheck each of them and go down the list, unchecking all the boxes that no longer serve you.

Then you place checks in front of the boxes that say "Think lovingly," "Accept myself as I am," "Life is safe," "I love what I am doing no matter what I am doing," and any other box that sounds good. Down at the bottom, you notice a box marked "Life is limitless," and you check that one as well.

In this chapter, you learned about the power of perspective, ways of enhancing your physical sense, and the value of enjoying the process. If you apply these concepts, you can make your life magical, special, and exactly what you want.

In the next chapter, we will focus on being more mindful and fully present in the moment.

Chapter 4

Mind Candy

How many things have you worried about in your life that never happened? How often do you worry about the future or have regrets about the past? Would you like to feel joyous and free no matter what is happening in your life?

The good news is there is an easy way to experience happiness and joy without changing your life drastically. You do have to change the way you think, but that's a lot easier than trying to rearrange all those ducks and get them in a row. Invariably the ducks move just before they are all lined up. If you allow yourself to become mindful, the ducks don't matter anymore. You'll be fully present in the moment and have the capacity to savor each and every moment of your life.

These meditations will help you feel the magic of the night, connect with your own innate wisdom, and learn how to quiet your restless mind.

Practicing Mindfulness

The meditations and the information in this book are designed to help you create all the ease, happiness, and joy you could possibly want. It is relatively easy to start thinking that your mind is the problem, or at the very least, your way of thinking is. Judgment doesn't help; gentleness, love, patience, and practice do.

Judging your mind just creates an internal tug of war. Judgment only creates more conflict. Shifting the way you look at life, changing your perspective helps you create greater peace of mind. As you become more mindful of your thoughts, your choices change. As you become aware of what is—how you habitually think about life—it is much easier to make choices that are consistent with creating what you really want. Mindfulness is a very powerful tool that will enable you to change your perspective, and in the process, change your experience of life.

Mindfulness is empowering as well as transformational. As you practice mindfulness, you intentionally focus your awareness on your thoughts and actions in the present moment in an accepting and nonjudgmental manner. Mindfulness can be applied gently to bodily actions and the mind's own thoughts and feelings. In Buddhism, mindfulness is considered a prerequisite for developing insight and wisdom.

How you think is a habit, and you can change your perspective with a bit of practice. I frequently use the word "allow" and the phrase "allow for the possibility." If you are willing to allow for the possibility, you open the door to new ways of thinking and the limitless possibilities life holds.

The simple act of *allowing* changes a lot. Are you willing to allow for the possibility that you can be deliriously happy, feel totally fulfilled, loved, accepted, and at peace?

It is possible! Just be mindful of your thoughts and align them with those feelings.

Pebbles in a Pond

Thoughts are like ripples on a pond. Ripples rise and fall, and then they slowly disappear. I find this meditation very restful, and it helps me realize how all my choices affect my experience of life.

You can use this meditation to relax and change the way you are feeling. As always, you can use the meditation to fill your life with peace and a sense of ease. Use your favorite induction before you start the meditation. Experiment with using different ones until one fits.

Imagine yourself standing beside a beautiful, peaceful pond. Majestic trees surround its edges, the air smells sweet and clean, and there is a gentle breeze. As you slowly and mindfully walk around the edge of the pond, butterflies float effortlessly along. The sky is full of fluffy clouds, and the air is a perfect temperature. You are moved by the beauty and serenity.

You walk along until you see an inviting bench. It is sitting at the end of a short, wide dock. The sun sinks lower in the sky, filling the land with long, graceful shadows. Dragonflies touch the surface of the water, creating ripples. You allow yourself to be filled with the peace and magic of this special place.

Next to the bench is a small pile of pebbles. They are beautiful little stones. Each one is unique and special. Slowly, one by one, you throw them into the pond. You watch the ripples as they emanate outward in ever-expanding circles. The ripples intersect and mingle in seemingly random patterns. As you watch the ripples, you realize they are much like your thoughts. Some are expanding, while others overlap, intersecting, connecting, and growing.

You realize that if you throw pebbles of peace into your life, you get more peace. If you think judgmental thoughts, you create judgment and fear. As you sit silently on that bench, you decide to throw pebbles of love into your life, and as you do, you effortlessly let go of your old thoughts of judgment and fear.

Slowly and gently bring yourself back to normal everyday awareness. You could stand up and stretch.

"Don'ts" Don't Work

Much like a computer, your mind is repetitive, repeating only what it already knows. Today, you will think 95 percent of the same thoughts you thought yesterday unless you consciously make new choices.

If I say to you, "Whatever you do, *don't* think about a beautiful, ripe red tomato," you automatically think of one. Just hearing the words brings up an image. At a profound level, the universe and our minds simply don't hear negatives. If you think, "I don't want to feel alone anymore," guess what? It is the same as saying, "I want to be lonely." If, instead, you focus on what you *do* want, you'll get more of that as well. Instead of saying, "I don't want to be lonely," think, "I want to feel loved or connected."

Giving yourself permission to know what you really want is a very big step toward creating a life full of freedom, happiness, peace of mind, and joy. The external world is temporary and constantly changing. If you expect something "out there" to bring you happiness, you are going about it the hard way. It's much easier to give yourself permission to have it regardless of external circumstances.

> If one advances confidently in the direction of his dreams, and endeavors to live the life he imagined, he will meet with a success unexpected in common hours.
>
> —Henry David Thoreau, writer and naturalist

If you want to feel loved, love yourself. If you want more money, explore what money means to you. If you believe having money will help you feel secure, then give yourself permission to feel secure whether you have money or not. Focus on what you do want, explore the reasons for the desire, and then decide if you are willing to allow yourself to have it.

Discovering Your Inner Sanctuary

This meditation helps you create a place within yourself where you feel safe and can connect with your innate, inner wisdom. Use it often until you can easily go to your inner sanctuary. It is a wonderful resource and a great place to go before you make major decisions in your life.

You can begin the meditation by thinking about looking at yourself in a mirror. Take a few deep breaths and relax.

See yourself standing in front of yourself. Imagine that self getting smaller and smaller. You are so tiny you can easily float upward and fly. You fly toward your forehead and walk directly into an opening right in the middle of your forehead. You stand there for a moment and then leap off into space, flying downward toward the very center of your being. The ride is exhilarating. You laugh with joy.

As you reach the core of your being, you find a very special place. It is your inner sanctuary. It is a place of peace, full of wisdom, where you can connect with yourself, recharge your spirit, and bask in the unconditional love that is the essence of who and what you really are.

You spend some time becoming familiar with your inner sanctuary. It can feel like a real place, or it can simply be a feeling. Decorate it. Fill it with whatever pleases you—mountains and streams, a fireplace, and an overstuffed chair. Fill it with lots of things or nothing at all. This is a place where you can connect with yourself and your own inner wisdom. To help you access that wisdom, you can create a library or a talking computer.

You can fill your sanctuary with other people or beings that can help you. Take some time and connect. Allow yourself to be filled with the magic and wonder that fills your sanctuary. Come here often.

Take a few deep breaths and bring yourself back. You might want to spend some time writing about your sanctuary. You could even find images to make your sanctuary more real.

Our true home is in the present moment. To live in the present moment is a miracle. The miracle is not to walk on water. The miracle is to walk on the green Earth in the present moment, to appreciate the peace and beauty that are available now. Peace is all around us—in the world and in nature—and within us—in our bodies and in our spirits. Once we learn to touch this peace, we will be healed and transformed. It is not a matter of faith; it is a matter of practice.

—Thich Nhat Hanh, Buddhist monk and author

The Only One Who Matters Is You

Have you ever had someone accuse you of being selfish? Being selfish has a negative connotation and is highly underrated. Being selfish is simply the act of putting yourself first, so you have more than enough love to share with other people. If Mother Teresa had shown up in India with no food and no resources, she certainly wouldn't have been able to feed the poor and help so many people. The most important person in your world is you. Imagine what life would be like if everyone took care of themselves, loved themselves unconditionally.

What if accepting yourself was a normal part of life? What if we were taught to ask clearly for what we wanted and needed? How much easier life would be. Everyone would have more than enough, so each person would have plenty to share.

Early in my journey, one of my mentors told me never to share of myself. I was shocked because he was a very loving, giving, caring man. He went on to say, make sure you always keep your own cup full and then share only of the overflow. He told me to make sure I always took care of my wants and needs, nurtured myself, and took time each day to connect with my spirit. He said then I would always have enough to share with others.

When you put yourself first, you have enough to share with the rest of the people in your life. If you are too busy to take care of yourself, you are too busy.

Sitting in the Middle of the Lake

This meditation is a great way to quiet your mind, especially during turmoil. You can use it whenever your thoughts begin creating unwanted waves in your life. Focusing on your breath is a great way to begin this meditation.

Imagine yourself sitting comfortably on the surface of the water in the middle of the lake. You are feeling totally calm, relaxed, and at peace.

It feels wonderful to be sitting on the water. You begin to notice that each of your thoughts causes a ripple on the surface of the water. As you calm your thoughts, the water's surface becomes totally still.

You allow yourself to play with the waves and your thoughts. You begin to think about something, and the waves lap at your feet. You think about something you find upsetting, and your body begins to rock with the waves. As you quiet your thoughts, the water begins to look like a mirror reflecting the clouds on its surface.

You breathe deeply and fill yourself with a deep sense of peace and ease. As you float on the surface of the water, you think thoughts that fill you with a sense of self-acceptance.

You see yourself effortlessly doing things for yourself, loving things, nurturing things that fill your inner cup to overflowing. You feel a profound sense of generosity, a connection to your spirit. You feel full and notice how wonderful it feels to openly share the overflow.

It feels so magical to give yourself what you want and need. It is a pleasure to do things for yourself, truly take care of yourself, and be selfish enough to love yourself.

You start to realize being selfish is an act of love and that being selfless is an action based on scarcity and fear.

Selflessness is not at all loving and often comes from a desire to be liked. So, you allow yourself to selfishly fill yourself up with love and acceptance until it fills every cell of your body and overflows into the world around you.

You sit back and enjoy the support of the water and the peace it brings you.

For me, it is far better to grasp the Universe as it really is than to persist in delusion, however satisfying and reassuring.

—Carl Sagan, astronomer and writer

Blowing in the Wind

Thoughts come and go. They are a lot like the wind. You can't see the wind directly, but you can watch as it moves the trees and the grass. You can feel the wind on your face. The wind can destroy property or be used to generate electricity. The wind is just the wind.

Life is just life. Everything in life is emotionally neutral. Something happens, and then we tell ourselves a story about what happened. It is our story that creates our emotional responses. Nothing in life is inherently good or bad. Of course, certain behaviors are more desirable than others. It is important for us to realize we create the emotions with our thoughts.

Taking responsibility for our emotional reactions gives us a great deal of freedom. We can choose how we want to feel rather than being a victim to a story about the events around us. We can learn to be happy regardless of what is happening around us.

Walking Mindfully

Walking mindfully can be a form of a walking meditation. It's very soothing to walk slowly, breathing fully, feeling each leg as it moves, noticing your foot as it rises and falls, and feeling how your legs support your weight. When you don't feel like going for a walk outside, you can go for a walk in this mystical forest.

Focus your attention on your feet. Wiggle your toes and feel your feet.

Imagine yourself standing under a canopy of trees. The path beneath your feet is moss covered, and sunlight gently filters through the leaves, creating shimmering areas of light. The forest is very quiet, filled only with the sound of the wind and the occasional bird celebrating life. The moss feels so soft and supportive underfoot.

Slowly pick up one leg and place it in front of you. Notice how it feels to walk slowly, shifting your weight from one leg to the other. Breathe deeply, filling your lungs with the smells of the forest and focusing your attention on the process of walking slowly along the path.

Stop for a moment and feel your body. Move your shoulders, rotate your head slowly, and wiggle your hips. Pick up one foot and balance on just one leg.

Feel your body as it engages various muscles to maintain your balance. Focus your thoughts and feelings mindfully on the process of moving your body from one place to another.

Think of a baby as he learns to walk. At first, he falls more often than he stands up. But with a bit of practice, he can walk and run and jump. Mindfully focus your attention on your ability to walk and allow yourself to stroll mindfully amongst the trees.

When you feel done, gently bring yourself back.

Remember, spiritual practices do require practice. The more often you practice them, the greater the benefits and the easier they become.

Give yourself the gift of playing with these meditations until you feel comfortable with them. It may take some practice to quiet your mind and allow yourself to play with your imagination, but I guarantee you will be glad you did!

The Moon and the Stars

Next time you bite into an apple, eat a piece of bread, or munch on your favorite food, practice eating it mindfully.

Imagine biting into your favorite food. Its flavor and texture fill your mouth. It tastes so good. You chew it slowly, savoring its flavor.

As you take another bite, think of all the people who made it possible.

Think about the farmers who grew all the ingredients, the people who picked the crops, the truckers who carried it, the people who built the trucks, and the people who refined the gas. Think of all the people who made your favorite food possible.

Now, think of the sun and the moon and the stars that fill each and every cell of the food. Slowly and mindfully savor your favorite food. Imagine the stars as they fill your body. And give thanks to all the people who made it possible.

In this chapter, we focused on practicing being mindful and playing with your physical sense to change your inner dialog more easily.

In the next chapter, we'll explore making life lighter, easier, and more fun.

Chapter 5

Lighten Up

Some people seek enlightenment in their search for happiness. Enlightenment means to illuminate, and it also refers to the highest spiritual state one can achieve. I think when anything becomes an external goal, it also becomes the source of pain rather than a path to happiness. If you need or want something to be happy, happiness will often remain elusive. Happiness is long-lasting when it comes from the inside out.

Depending on which version you read, Buddha is attributed with saying that the root of all suffering is attachment, desire, the disturbed mind, or ignorance. I have found that anything that lessens our connection with the essence of our spirit and who and what we are causes suffering. It's so easy to get too serious about almost anything.

Trial and error is the only way to know what's important to you, your connection to your spirit, and what helps you connect with the essence of who and what you are. You are the energy that gives life to your body.

Having a direct experience with inner peace is far different from reading about it, even if the words are beautiful and resonate with you. Take a deep breath and continue to lightly tread on your path toward your own inner happiness, peace, and joy.

You are not your body. You are the spirit that resides inside your body. Every breath is a gift of life from your spirit. The more you connect with your spirit, the more magical your life becomes.

Laughter as Medicine

When we laugh, our bodies go through all sorts of physiological changes. Our blood pressure lowers, our muscles relax, and our oxygen levels increase. On average, a child laughs 300 times a day while an adult only laughs 17. Using your sense of humor is a wonderful way to relieve stress and feel better about life.

The two meditations that follow will help you embrace the joy of living. You could also binge watch some funny movies or sitcoms. Do some of the activities that create a feeling of ease, joy, love, and laughter.

To help add joy to your life, keep a list of activities that you enjoy doing. I had a list in the back of my daily journal, and I referred to it often when I was in a mood. At first, I had nothing on my list, and then by experimenting I added more and more things. I learned to play a Native American flute and allowed myself to enjoy learning how to play. I used to think I hated movies and then one day I went to see the movie *Ghost* and enjoyed myself. Experiment, and if you find something on your list that seems like a chore, erase it.

> ## Nothing is good or bad. It is thinking that makes it so.
>
> —William Shakespeare, poet and dramatist

Raining Joy

This meditation is a simple but powerful way to change how you are feeling at any given moment. Use your favorite induction or just breathe and relax.

Imagine you are curled up, sitting on a window seat. You are quietly looking out at a peaceful, rainy day.

The water drops slide down the windowpane, creating little rainbows as the light from the room passes through them. The wind blows, and for a moment, the rain pelts against the window. You feel very peaceful, safe, and comfortable. You begin to drift off to sleep and find yourself dreaming.

You are walking outside in the middle of a rainstorm. Your first instinct is to run back inside, but you notice the rain isn't wet at all. As you look at the raindrops, you begin to feel like laughing.

You are filled with joy, and you realize it is raining joy. You are not sure how or why, but you take a deep breath and allow the joy to fill your heart and your mind.

You stand in the rain, hold your hands over your head, and just dance for the sheer pleasure of it. Allow yourself to be filled to overflowing with joy.

Slowly bring yourself back and take a few moments to write about your experience.

Twinkle, Twinkle, Little Star

Over the centuries, the stars, moon, and sun have fascinated human beings, inspiring impressive structures like Stonehenge.

Have you ever looked up at the stars and wondered what you were doing on this little speck of dust called Earth? Or made a wish upon a star? The light from some of the stars we see has been traveling for hundreds of years. Some of the stars we see no longer exist. Your body is made of stardust.

What's all this got to do with your life? It is all about perspective. Change your perspective, and your life changes. An ancient spiritual teacher once said, "Before speaking, consider whether it is an improvement upon silence." That concept can also apply to your thinking.

Some great questions to ask yourself on a regular basis are …

- Is that thought going to improve my life?
- Does that thought or action enlighten my life?
- Does that train of thought make my life lighter and more joyful?
- Does my perspective or opinion make me happy?

If the answer to any of those questions is no, simply change your thoughts.

Some of the stars you see in the night sky no longer exist, yet there they are. Most of your beliefs are based on assumptions you made when you were a young child. Those assumptions may no longer be valid. Perhaps it is time to let them go and see life in a way that supports a greater sense of happiness and joy instead.

Watching the Stars

This meditation helps you change the way you look at life. Remember, small changes eventually lead to big ones. Find a comfortable place where you won't be disturbed, and relax.

The night is dark, and the air crisp and cool. You go outside and look up. There are millions and millions of stars shining down upon you. You don't ever remember seeing so many stars before. You walk over to a comfortable lounge chair and lie down, looking up at the stars. You put your hands behind your head and relax.

The sky is black, and the stars twinkle magically. There is a timeless quality to them, with no beginning and no end. You look into the infinity of space. As you watch a falling star streak across the sky, you feel connected to everyone and everything. You take a deep breath, wish upon a star, and know all things are possible.

You spend a few more minutes looking up, and for a moment, you wonder who is looking at you. You smile, and your sense of connectedness deepens.

Take a few deep breaths and focus your attention on your surroundings.

Only You Can Light Up Your Life

Your thoughts and opinions can create great joy or intense misery and anything in between. Saying "I know" limits your ability to see other possibilities.

Once you think, "I know," instead of continuing to be curious about how else you can see a situation, you are smack dab in the middle of your old limiting thinking.

There is a big difference between wisdom and knowledge. Wisdom springs from within us. It is the voice of our spirits. Once we think, "I know," our minds are closed to other possibilities.

We cling to our own points of view, as though everything depended on it. Yet our opinions have no permanence; like autumn and winter, they gradually pass away.

—Chuang Tzu, philosopher

When you hear yourself say, "I know," why not follow that thought with the questions:

"How else can I see this?"
"How could I see this through the eyes of love?"

For example, if you are late and your friend points that out, what if instead of saying "I know" or "I'm sorry," you explore how being late serves you?

Candles Around the World

Allowing your light to shine invites others to do the same. The more supported you feel, the more loved you feel, the easier it is for you to let go of your old limiting beliefs. When like-minded people encourage you, it makes change even easier. This meditation assists you in feeling the magic and wonder of love.

You find yourself facing a beautiful altar, lit by one candle. The flickering light coming from the candle fills you with a deep sense of gratitude and love.

You watch the flames as they grow bigger and seem to dance. Your eyes move toward the shadows flickering on the wall. The shadows are beautiful. One clearly looks like an angel reaching out to hug you.

One by one, people slowly come up to the altar, stand for a moment, and light their candles. After a time, you approach the altar and light your candle as well. As you light your candle, you realize that lighting all those other candles in no way diminishes the original candle.

You turn and watch as people slowly share their light with others until the entire world is bathed in the gentle glow. In your mind's eye, you see yourself sharing your love with someone and that person sharing it with someone else until a single act of kindness circles the globe.

You send out ripples of peace and love and watch them as they expand and grow. Imagine those ripples flowing forward in time, creating ease and harmony in your life, enabling you to make all your decisions effortlessly.

Take a few minutes to write about your experience and allow yourself to savor the peace and love.

Make a Wish and Blow Out the Candles

I love this story:

> A young girl and her mother were walking along the beach. There were thousands of starfish washed up on the shore. The little girl began picking them up and throwing them back in the water.
> The mother said, "Don't bother; it won't make a difference."
> The little girl thought for a moment, looking at the one in her hand. "It will to this one."

You can always make a difference in the moment, choice by choice and thought by thought.

Every day can be your birthday. You can start over at any moment. If you could start all over, what would you change? Take a few minutes to think about that before you read this meditation.

One of the things I like doing on my birthday is to write a letter to the universe. I start out by reflecting on the past year and giving thanks for all the experiences I had. Then I write about what I would like to create in the coming year. I go out in nature, watch the sunrise, and read my letter out loud. Then I put it away someplace where I will run across it sometime in the future. Even a few months later, it is fun to read what I have written.

You are standing in front of a huge birthday cake. There are many candles, and all the people you have ever known stand on the other side of the cake. They are all here to wish you well, share their love, and support you as you begin your new life. Even people with whom you've had difficult relationships smile at you lovingly.

You take a deep breath and look at the candlelight reflected in everyone's eyes. The reflection reminds you of a starlit night.

The magic and love of the moment fills your heart and your mind. You think about what you want to let go of, and you imagine it being transformed by the flames dancing before you.

Next, you take another deep breath and think about what you would like to fill your life with. You breathe in the joy, ease, magic, and miracles you are inviting into your life.

You look around again at all your friends and family, and they smile at you, nodding their heads. When you feel ready, you take a deep breath and blow out all the candles. A loud cheer breaks out, laughter fills the room, and you know your wishes are just a thought away.

Relax back into your life, bringing a smile and the magical wonder back with you.

> If you have made mistakes ... there is always another chance for you ... you may have a fresh start any moment you choose, for this thing we call "failure" is not the falling down, but the staying down.
>
> —Mary Pickford, star of silent films

Circle of Friends

At one level, we are all connected, yet it is easy to feel alone. This is a wonderful meditation to remind you of that connection and help you remember you are loved. No one can walk your path for you, but you can certainly invite supportive and loving people to share your process. Take a moment to relax before you begin.

You are walking along a beautiful path, leading through an ancient forest. The air smells fresh and clean. The wind stirs, and you feel yourself embraced by the loving presence of all the spirits in this sacred forest. You feel a deep sense of reverence and awe. Off in the distance, you hear birds singing and a brook as it tumbles over the moss-covered rocks. You feel totally safe, loved, and at peace.

The path is soft underfoot. As the sunlight filters through the canopy of trees, it creates sparkles of shimmering light. You move effortlessly along. You notice a fork in the trail, and you stop for a moment while you feel the energy of each path. You take a deep breath and allow your awareness to sink into the core of your being.

You imagine walking down each path. One feels more loving and expansive, so you walk confidently down it.

Up ahead, there is a clearing. As you walk into the clearing, it takes a moment for your eyes to adjust to the bright light. When you look around, you see many other men and women gathering in the clearing. You realize you've entered what is best described as a circle of friends.

Standing there, you hear laughter and joy. At a profound level, you realize you are in the presence of incredible wisdom. You take a deep breath and step into the center of the circle. One by one, each person comes and stands in front of you.

They look deeply into your eyes and say, "You are loved, you are lovable, and you are love."

You feel the words deep in your heart and allow their love to flow into you. Their love touches you at a profound level. You know what it feels like to be loved unconditionally. As a tear slowly finds its way down your cheek, you are filled with a sense of peace, ease, and joy.

Letting Go of Fear

I used to have a bumper sticker that said, "Commit random acts of kindness and senseless acts of beauty." Maybe today, you can put money in someone else's parking meter or pay his toll. While standing in line at Starbucks, pay for the person behind you.

One time, I put dollar bills on people's windshields. It only cost me a few dollars, but I felt like a million dollars after doing it. It is a wonderful way to change the way you feel and see life from another perspective.

Fear is:

F false
E evidence
A appearing
R real

I have taught people how to walk on red hot, burning coals without burning themselves. (I certainly wouldn't recommend that you try this at home unless you like to barbeque, but it is possible with training!) We can suspend the laws of physics if we allow ourselves to be fully focused in the present moment.

Think about your greatest fear. What one thing are you most afraid of having happen? Is it illness? Being homeless? Dying all alone? Living all alone? What is your greatest fear?

Play it out in your mind. Imagine what it would be like to be living that experience. Make it as real as possible. Feel it, live it, and be it. Now ask yourself if it is something you really want to create. Is that what you really want in your life?

Chances are, the answer is a resounding no. Imagine tying that fear to a big, colorful helium balloon and watching it float harmlessly away. Just let it go.

Now think about what you do want to create. What would you like to create instead? Think about it, feel it, and allow it to be real for you. Now imagine that image getting bigger and bigger until it fills your entire vision. Then let it go, see it spinning and swirling around until it, too, moves off into space. And know it is so.

If your old fear comes back, attach it to a balloon, let it go, and watch it float away. Then, once again, focus on what you do want to create.

In this chapter, I invited you to redefine fear, to remember you have a circle of friends in spirit, if not physically, and to feel the magic of wishing on a star. Your life can be as magical as you allow it to be. Rewrite your thoughts, and allow the magic to begin.

In the next chapter, we explore ways you can make your life really good, grand even.

Chapter 6

Life Is Grand

Life can be just as wonderful as you are willing to allow it to be. You can celebrate what is or focus on what isn't. Is the glass half empty or half full? When you watch children play, they get totally lost in worlds that don't even exist for adults. Happiness really is only a thought away.

Life is filled with endless possibilities. Your choices and how you choose to see life makes all the difference. In the 1930s, during the Great Depression, more people became millionaires than at any other time in history. However, many families lost everything they owned. So, what was the difference?

Everything in our lives is either there or not there based on what we think and believe. It isn't that the families that lost everything did something wrong, while the millionaires did something right. It's just a matter of different belief systems. You can look at life and see tragedy, or you can see opportunities to share your love and your light.

You can use your imagination to create anything you want. Life is magical if you are willing to see the magic in it all. Life can be mundane or magical, depending on your perspective. The meditations in this chapter will help you realize how incredibly powerful your perspective is and help you open up to the magical possibilities life holds.

Imagine That!

Imagination is our ability to create new images and different combinations of thoughts and feelings. Imagined images are seen with the "mind's eye," and imagination is free of objective restraints. We can use imagination to create worlds of fiction and make progress in scientific exploration.

The more you engage your imagination in a positive way, the better your life will become. What if you were able to look at life and see the perfection in everything? Instead of wanting to change the world, what if you accepted the world, your life, and yourself just as it is? Acceptance facilitates change, while judgment acts like cosmic superglue.

Whatever you judge adheres to your conscious awareness. When you judge something, you are once again saying, "Don't think about a red fire truck." You must think about the fire truck to *not* think about it.

I have been studying with a *kupuna* (Hawaiian elder). She learned the ancient wisdom of her people from her grandfather, and she talks about living "aloha." As a visitor, you are told the word *aloha* is a greeting that means hello or goodbye. In the ancient Hawaiian tradition (that has nothing to do with Huna), aloha is a way of life. When you live aloha, you live with an open heart, a loving mind, and a generosity of spirit. You are loving, gentle, and quietly powerful. You have the ability to freely share. I have heard it said that when a person who lives aloha smiles, you can see his or her spirit.

The ancient Hawaiians talk about everything being *pono*, a word that roughly translates to "perfect." When you see the world through the eyes of love, "everything is pono until you think otherwise." If you are willing, you can decide to start seeing life as pono. You'll be amazed at what happens.

The only thing that is real is love; everything else is an illusion or delusion of our minds. The author of "A Course in Miracles" (acim.org) says everything is either love or a call for love.

So, if there is something in your life you don't see as perfect, imagine it is your opportunity to live aloha and send it your love instead of your judgment.

> Imagination is the beginning of creation. You imagine what you desire; you will what you imagine; and at last you create what you will.
> —George Bernard Shaw, dramatist and critic

Listening to Your Heart

Often your mind will tell you one thing while your heart intuits something else. You had the feeling you should bring a jacket, but you didn't, so you were cold or wet. Or you're sitting around thinking about someone, then the telephone rings, and it is the person you were thinking about? That's your intuition working.

We all have a filter system. It is composed of all of our beliefs, agreements, assumptions, and attitudes about life. We never see life directly. We see a distorted version of life based on our filter system. The trick to being truly happy, no matter what is happening in your life, is to realize you can change your perspective. Be willing to let go of any limiting pieces of your filter system and decide to see the perfection in what already is.

Has your mind asked you yet whether denying reality is denial? It isn't. We deny reality all the time by demanding to see it through the distorted vision of our filter system.

Cosmic Waterfall

Your perspective determines your experience. This meditation allows you to see how powerful your perspective really is.

Use your favorite induction, sit where you won't be bothered, and slip into a relaxed state.

You've spent your entire life living in a beautiful cave right behind a huge waterfall. The air is wet, and everything is blurry on the other side.

There is a constant roar as the water pours over the face of the cave into the abyss below. It feels safe and familiar in the cave. You and your friends like it. You can go anyplace if it is inside of the cave.

One day, you wake up, and it's quiet. You look out and beyond the cave's walls. It is very bright, and the opening is huge. You see the sky clearly for the first time. It is blue with fluffy white clouds floating along.

You step out of the cave and realize there is a whole world just beyond the waterfall. There is an entirely different world beyond the cave, beyond the previous limits of your existence.

You run out into the sunshine and feel its warmth on your skin. It feels glorious. The colors of the flowers are so vibrant, and the smells are incredible.

As you explore this new world, you are amazed you stayed in that small cave so long. You are grateful that you finally got to see the world beyond your cave.

The water begins to flow over the cliff again, but you decide to stay and explore this new world instead. You have decided to no longer live life from behind your filter system anymore.

Great ideas come into the world as quietly as doves. Perhaps then, if we listen attentively, we shall hear among the uproar of empires and nations a faint fluttering of wings, the gentle stirrings of life and hope.

—Albert Camus, writer

Hot Air Balloon

Beyond the repetitious thoughts of your mind lies the innate wisdom of your spirit. The voice of your spirit is like a quiet whisper, while your mind is much more like a raucous crow. Learning to listen to the whispers takes practice. Trust the process. Allow yourself to hear the quiet whispers of your spirit.

As you read this meditation, remind yourself you can hear the message your heart has for you. You *can* hear the message from your spirit.

You are sitting on the side of a hill, looking down at the valley. The gently rolling hills look like a series of well-manicured lawns. The sky is a brilliant blue. It is a sunny day, there is a gentle breeze, and the temperature is perfect for you.

As you sit there enjoying the day, you notice something colorful coming over the ridge. At first, you aren't sure what it is, and then you realize it is a rainbow-colored hot air balloon. As the balloon floats effortlessly along, you notice the basket under it seems to be empty. When it begins to land on a hill nearby, you run over.

As it settles down, you walk up to it and look in the basket. There is a little creature in there. You aren't sure what it is, but it looks friendly, and its eyes are full of love.

He hands you a huge, empty cardboard box and in a soft voice, tells you to put anything that no longer serves you into it. He invites you to put all your limiting beliefs, old emotions, and memories into the box. He lovingly explains that you can let go of all that old stuff and open your heart to a more expansive, loving way of looking at the world.

He hands you as many boxes as you need. You fill up box after box. When you are done, you hand all the boxes back to the creature. To your surprise, they all fit back into the basket.

You look into his eyes, and you feel incredibly loved, safe, accepted, and free. He smiles and waves goodbye as the hot air balloon slowly takes off.

*You watch as the balloon and your friend slowly drift upward.
You put your hand above your eyes so you can see it more clearly.
Suddenly, a small box comes sailing out of the basket. You race
over and pick it up. It has a little tag with your name on it. You open
it, and there is a small, handwritten note inside with a message just
for you.*

Take some time as you slowly come back, from the meditation, and make
sure you write your message down.

Early on in my journey, I used to have notes written on paper all over the
place. Then, one day, I began using index cards. Index cards can help you
transform your filter system. When I was retraining my mind, I bought a
pack of index cards and wrote a variety of quotes on them.

When I started thinking in my habitual fashion, I'd read my index cards
until I started thinking in a more expansive way. Try making your own
set of index cards. There are many great quotes in this book to get you
started. You could also use the book by opening it randomly and reading
meditations until your mind changes tunes.

Savor All of Life

Rainbows require both rain and sunshine to exist. There are times here
on the Big Island of Hawaii when it will rain for weeks on end. It is easy
to get tired of the rain when everything in the house is damp, and you
haven't seen the sun for weeks. Judging the rain doesn't change anything,
but if I embrace it, I can enjoy it.

When a relationship ends or you lose your job, it is hard to enjoy
the experience and think that it's perfect. Life is an emotionally rich
experience. We can learn to savor it all instead of trying to avoid the "bad
times" and hang on to the "good times." No matter how hard it is raining,
the sky is clear on the other side of the clouds.

Every event is an opportunity for us to deepen our connection to our
filter system or our spirit. We can label things as good and bad or positive
and negative, or we can savor all of life. A shimmering diamond is made

of carbon, just like a lump of coal. We can use life to polish the facets of our hearts and learn to love unconditionally.

Savoring everything in life is merely a decision we make in the moment. Heaven or hell are always only a thought away.

You've Got Rainbows

To do this meditation, you can look in a mirror or imagine looking into one. It helps you feel better about yourself and realize what a miracle you really are.

Look at yourself in a mirror. Look deep into your eyes and see the beauty of your spirit reflected there. As you look at yourself lovingly, think about what a miracle it is that you even exist.

Your mother and father had to meet and give birth to you. Their parents had to meet and give birth to your mom and dad.

The mathematical improbability of your existence is astronomical. You are a miracle. There is only one of you, and without you, the universe would be incomplete.

As you look at yourself, you see a beautiful rainbow forming over your head. The colors are bright and vibrant. The rainbow swirls around you, filling you with a sense of love, peace, and joy. You breathe in the magic and wonder at all the colors. You are amazed at what you are seeing. How wonderful it is that you have rainbows.

Smile deeply, and bring yourself back.

A human being is a part of the whole called by us "Universe," a part limited in time and space. He experiences himself, his thoughts, and feelings as something separated from the rest, a kind of optical delusion of his consciousness. This delusion is a kind of prison for us, restricting us to our personal desires and to affection for a few persons nearest to us. Our task must be to free ourselves from this prison by widening our circle of compassion to embrace all living creatures and the whole of nature in its beauty.

—Albert Einstein, physicist

Sunrise and Sunset

This world is so incredibly beautiful. It is such a rich, sensual planet. The sights, sounds, and smells are amazing, and the gift of life is something to be grateful for every moment of our existence.

When emotions are running rampant, getting out in nature can be very calming and healing. Imagine you're sitting quietly while watching a sunrise and sunset, giving thanks for another day, and reminding yourself you can fill it with whatever you want.

Your mind can take you there and set you free, or you can go for a ride on your limiting thoughts and your emotions. You are always free to choose, but only after you give yourself permission to choose.

You are sitting high on a bluff at the edge of the desert. The wind rustles the brush as it races across the dry landscape. The night is dark, but you can see clearly because the sky is filled with stars.

You sit facing the east. Slowly, ever so slowly, the horizon begins to get lighter. At first, there is a thin sliver of orange light that gradually turns pink. The sky above the horizon is a deep indigo. As you watch the horizon change colors, you are filled with a sense of wonder and awe at the beginning of a new day.

You take a deep breath and watch the morning stars shimmer, fading and growing brighter as the sun takes over. The sky continues to get brighter and brighter. The sun begins to peek over the horizon. It rapidly becomes a brilliant yellow globe warming the landscape.

As the sun clears the horizon, you say a silent prayer and give thanks for a new day and the opportunity to fill it with love, joy, and happiness. You sit and allow yourself to be filled with the beauty of the sun and the land around you.

You have an amazing day filled with magic, peace, joy, and laughter. You feel a profound sense of gratitude.

At the end of the day, you are magically transported to the ocean, where you watch the sun slowly sink into the water. The towering clouds turn pink and glow. As the sun sinks into the water, it creates diamonds of light that shimmer and dance. You see an amazing green flash of light as the sun sinks into the ocean.

As you reflect over the day, you give thanks for all the opportunities to see the gifts of life instead of judging what came your way. You are filled with love and gratitude for choosing to see life differently. What a gift it is to realize you can choose your thoughts moment by moment. Life really is perfect after all.

You might want to take some time and write about the experience.

Every day, God gives us the sun and also one moment in which we have the ability to change everything.

—Paulo Coelho, author

Field of Sunflowers

Sunflowers turn and follow the sun all day. They are big and bright, and it is amazing to watch these huge flowers as they move throughout the day.

Our emotions follow our thoughts, and our thoughts do change depending upon how we focus our attention. You can use this meditation to focus your thoughts or to focus your attention in a new, more expansive way.

You are walking down a country road at the end of summer when you come upon a whole field of sunflowers. They tower over your head and seem to go on forever. You sit by the side of the road and notice how they are all facing the sun.

You decide to sit down and relax. You lie down with the sun at your back, and the sunflowers are all looking away from you.

Some of the flower heads are over a foot across. They are huge and stand proudly in the field. You doze off for a while, and when you awaken, the sun is shining in your face. You look up, and the sunflowers all seem to be looking at you. You are amazed. You sit and watch for a while and see the sunflowers continue their daily journey.

You take a deep breath and think about how your emotions follow your thoughts. If you focus on fear, you create more fear. If you think loving and accepting thoughts, you create more of those as well. You breathe in love and acceptance and breathe out anything unlike it. You sit and take in the beauty of the acres and acres of sunflowers. You think about all the blessings in your life and smile. Life really is grand.

Writing a gratitude list on a regular basis is a wonderful practice, and now would be a great time to make one.

Life in a Pond

Ponds are incredible ecosystems. Unless polluted by humans, they are self-sustaining and naturally balance themselves. This is a great meditation to help you feel loved and to quiet your mind.

You find yourself sitting in the middle of a huge lily pad. It is early morning, and the frogs are still singing.

There are dozens of water lily buds standing proudly. As you look over the edge of your lily pad, you see lots of small fishes swimming around.

When they see your shadow, they dive deep into the pond. The sun strikes the water, and you watch dozens of pink water lilies open and greet the day.

As you watch the petals unfold, you feel your heart open and fill with love. You take a deep breath and watch as dragonflies drift by, just touching the surface of the water.

You watch water spiders dart around, seemingly walking on water. You are fascinated with all the different life forms that inhabit the pond.

As you watch in awe, you realize you are no longer sitting on the lily pad. You are standing beside the pond and smile at the gift you have just been given.

In this chapter, you received a message from a magical being in a hot air balloon and, in the process, realized how easy it is to get messages when you need them. You used your imagination to sit in a field of sunflowers and realized you do have rainbows.

You are magical! Your imagination really can set you free or bind you to your limitations. The choice is yours. These meditations are a wonderful way to practice setting yourself free.

In the next chapter, you will begin to focus on how wonderful your life can be (and already is).

Chapter 7

Making Your Heart Sing

What is it you absolutely love doing? What do you enjoy more than anything else? What if you were able to create that level of enjoyment with everything you do in your world? Would your life change drastically?

Living life passionately is your birthright. You really can be happy no matter what is happening in your life. You are the only one who can make your heart sing. The events in your life don't do that, but you can.

I used to think my grandfather was sweet but pretty much an old-fashioned fool before I understood the wisdom he so freely shared. He used to tell me that if you are a street sweeper, make sure you are the best street sweeper there is and put your whole heart into it. Years later, I realized that was also the key to enjoying every moment of my life. I don't sweep streets, but I do put my whole heart into everything I do, even sweeping the floor.

The meditations in this chapter help you focus on your connection to yourself. They assist you in feeling free and safe enough to be yourself, and help you realize how wonderful life can really be.

Happiness Is a Choice

The only person who can deny you your happiness is you. That seems like such an outlandish statement, yet it is true. Granted, there are certain definitions of words and concepts that everyone might agree upon, but only you can enforce the rules of your beliefs. You define what "makes" you happy and what doesn't.

It helps to realize that your mind would rather be right than happy. We often maintain our limiting perspective at the expense of our freedom and happiness. You can decide you will only be happy if _____, or you can decide to be happy right here and right now.

You can take singing lessons and practice for years or enjoy singing loudly and off-key. You can allow your life to be perfect just the way it is, and you can still lovingly decide to change something.

You can move away from unhappiness, but the problem is, you will only create more unhappiness to move away from. If instead, you embrace what is, change your thoughts and feelings, and learn to make new choices, you move toward greater freedom, happiness, and joy.

Dancing by the Light of the Moon

This meditation can fill you with the love and magic of a moonlit night. The moon is often equated with the power of the divine feminine and the goddess's magic.

I'm curious—have you decided yet which of the inductions or lead-ins to the meditations are your favorite and the most effective yet? Make sure you use them before each meditation. It makes the meditation more effective, easier, and fun.

The moon shines brightly overhead. It illuminates everything creating beautiful shadows. The light is so bright you walk effortlessly along a path as it winds through an ancient forest. You feel a sense of reverence and awe as you move silently through the ancient trees.

Off in the distance, you see a clearing and begin moving rapidly toward it. You find yourself moving faster and faster, almost running as you approach the clearing.

As you step into the circular clearing, you are almost moved to tears. The beauty and sense of belonging touch you deeply.

The moonlight sparkles off the ground, and you can feel the magic and power of the night. Love and acceptance flow through you. The moonlight sparkles all around you.

You remove your shoes and run through the grass, feeling incredibly free. You dance with joy. You move freely, leaping and twirling. You sing at the top of your voice. You have never felt freer.

The moon fills you with magic and wonder. You stand in the center of the circle and give thanks for the gifts of the night. You bow your head and ask for assistance in carrying these feelings with you into your life.

In your heart, you feel the answer: "As you wish, and so it is."

Take some time to come fully back to present moment focus and savor the feelings.

Keep your thoughts positive because your thoughts become your words. Keep your words positive because your words become your behaviors. Keep your behaviors positive because your behaviors become your habits. Keep your habits positive because your habits become your values. Keep your values positive because your values become your destiny.

—Mahatma Gandhi, spiritual and political leader

The Cosmic Choir

Finding your true inner voice—the loving, kind voice—and speaking your truth is very empowering.

Singing and making noise can be extremely freeing, even if it can be a bit intimidating. This meditation gives you an opportunity to experience the power of your voice and helps you find your own song.

Take your time relaxing before you do this meditation.

You find yourself on a huge stage surrounded by hundreds of people. Below you, there is an orchestra, and the musicians all seem to be tuning up their instruments. Each person only seems to be listening to their own instruments, paying little or no attention to the people around them.

People around you begin to hum.

At first, you feel a bit foolish, but then you look at the faces of the people around you. The look of freedom and joy makes you realize how much you long to sing your own song. As everyone sings their own song, the voices sound so beautiful together.

You realize you have always wanted to sing your own song and that your song is beautiful, it is unique, and it belongs to you. No one can sing your song but you.

As you join everyone and sing your song, your heart rejoices, and you sing even louder. At a deep level, you realize the universe would be incomplete without you.

Sit with this experience, relax, and really allow it to resonate with your inner being. Take it in and let it fill you with love, joy, and an inner knowledge of just how special you are.

What Do You Want?

When I ask people what they want, they usually give me a list of what they *don't* want. I don't want to feel lonely anymore. I don't want to struggle financially. I don't want to feel stressed or overwhelmed.

Practice asking yourself, "What do I want right now?" When you find yourself saying what you don't want, think about what it is you do want. Always focus your attention on what you want with the understanding that, at some level, you already have it. If you didn't, you would have no reason to desire it.

The Three Boxes

Allow yourself to be filled with a sense that life is perfect just as it is and that you are loved, safe, and nurtured—now and always. This meditation helps you realize that what you ask for can show up in a variety of ways, and what really matters is your acceptance. Take a moment to relax, breath deeply, and allow—just allow.

All your life, you have wanted to feel loved. One night, a magic genie shows up and gives you three wishes. Your first wish is to be loved. The genie raises their hand over your head; you hear a popping sound, and then the genie hands you a beautiful yellow box. As soon as you open it, you feel this incredible feeling of love well up, filling your heart. The love fills you up until all traces of loneliness, self-judgment, and isolation leave you. You feel whole and complete.

At first, you are grateful, but then you remember that feeling was supposed to come in the form of a loving relationship. You look at the genie and say, "I wanted a relationship, a partner to share my life with. That isn't what I wanted!"

The genie looks puzzled, but once again hands you a beautiful box wrapped in green. It looks too small to hold a person, but you unwrap it anyway. Poof—a person pops out of the box and immediately starts telling you they love you.

They fawn all over you and keep moving closer and closer. They can't seem to get enough of you. To your surprise, you feel smothered. You can't wait to get away from them.

You tell the genie that isn't what you want, either. The genie looks very sad and reminds you this is your last wish. There is a beautiful blue box behind the genie's back. The genie tells you it has the key to your happiness, but to accept it, you must be willing to let go of your expectations.

You reluctantly nod your head and take the box. You tear off the wrapping, and inside, there is a slip of paper. It says, "When love shows up in a yellow box, embrace it and accept it, even if you think it should show up in a green one."

Relax and allow yourself to slowly come back to everyday, waking awareness.

Being Supported

This fun meditation helps you experience support in a profound way.

You are a dolphin swimming rapidly through the water. The ocean is immense, and it effortlessly supports you.

The ocean provides your every want and need. Your body is sleek and strong. With a flip of your tail, you leap into the air, spinning, and feeling the freedom of your magnificent body.

You splash back into the water and dash off. You look at your shadow on the ocean's bottom as you effortlessly glide through the water.

The water is so deep and blue. It is abundant in everything. Friends surround you. Small ones frolic, dashing in and out of the pod. As your head barely breaks the surface, you take a deep breath of the life-giving air and dive to the depths below.

The sunlight swirls in magical vortexes. Shadows flit here and there, and you feel joyful.

Grandfather turtle is resting on the bottom, and you stop by to say hello. He greets you with his love. Off in the distance, you hear whales singing. You hear a boat's engine and decide to go play in its wake.

Magic and miracles are a matter of perspective, and you give thanks for the perspective.

Dream Big

Our imaginations are very powerful. What we believe is what we'll see and what our experiences will be based on. John Lennon wrote a beautiful song called "Imagine." Whether you've heard it or not, I invite you to take the time to listen, feel the words, and let them move you.

What kind of a world would you like to imagine? What would utopia look like to you? What would your role be in that world? What would the world be like if everyone took the time to do his or her emotional healing? Join me in creating that world, one person at a time.

Imagining a Peaceful World

If you want to create peace, it begins with you. This meditation is a wonderful visualization for world peace and for when you are feeling out of sorts or upset.

Imagine yourself standing in the center of a beautiful clearing in an ancient forest. The air smells fresh and clean, heavy with the musky smell of wet earth after a gentle rain.

You begin slowly walking around the clearing. It feels familiar and safe. You find yourself surrounded by the energy of love. A shaft of light fills the clearing with a magical light.

Slowly, people begin to fill the clearing. As each one enters, they reach out and hug you. You feel full and connected and at peace.

Before long, the entire clearing is full of people holding each other's hands, sharing love, and feeling connected and at peace. You look around at the faces; they are all different ages, races, shapes, and sizes.

You look around and notice their hearts are beaming with light. A beautiful pink light emanates from their hearts, joining with the light of those around them.

You see mental images of them moving through their lives, making all of their choices based on love. They are free of fear; you are free of fear. Love guides your way; love surrounds you and fills your very being.

You see a world in which everyone is so full of love they are free of fear. It is a world in which all people realize they are one, in which all people make their choices based on love and mutual respect.

It is a world free of hatred, free of prejudice. The air is clear and the water clean. Everyone, including the heads of state and the leaders of industry, makes their decisions based on the good of the planet and all people, great and small.

Take a few moments to envision that world and then know it could be even more magnificent than you could possibly imagine.

Allow it to be grand, glorious, and free. Imagine your life in that world. Imagine yourself doing what you love as your livelihood. Imagine all your wants and needs being effortlessly met. Imagine that for everyone everywhere in the world.

Imagine all people living in peace and harmony. Imagine a world of love. Imagine a world that is safe, loving, supportive, and nurturing to all its inhabitants.

Now let it be so. Let that world take form in your mind and begin to materialize in your life.

Paradise is exactly like where you are right now, only much, much better.

—William Seward Burroughs, author

The Magic Wand

For this mediation, imagine finding a magic wand that allows you to create whatever you want, when you want it. Do this meditation often, and you'll have that experience.

You open one of the drawers in your bedroom, and you see something very unusual. It looks like a stick, but when you pick it up, your hand tingles. When you move it around, sparkling bits of dust swirl in the air.

As you look closer, the dust looks like tiny stars, shimmering and glowing. You shake the wand, and an avalanche of stardust spews forth.

You think to yourself, "I wonder what this is?" Poof! A small book appears. On the cover in gold letters are the words, "How to Use a Magic Wand."

The reality of it begins to wash over you. You have a magic wand, and you can do anything you want, create anything you want, and change your life in any way you want.

The instruction book says you can only use it on yourself and your life. It doesn't work on others or the world out there. But it says you can change anything you want with it.

You hold the magic wand close to your heart, and you give thanks for the opportunity to remember what a magical being of light you are.

You realize that there has always been a magic wand in the center of your heart, just waiting for you to use it. That magic wand is called love and acceptance. Love will enable you to create anything you want whenever you want it.

Sit quietly for a moment allowing the magic to sink slowly into your awareness. Bring the magic, love, and laughter back with you.

Being Good to Yourself

If you don't take care of yourself, who will? You deserve to take all the time necessary to nurture yourself, take care of your wants and needs, prepare nutritious meals, have a beautiful home, have a job you feel passionate about, and have enough time to relax and just enjoy life. You deserve to have a love affair with yourself.

If you like getting cards, then go to the store, pick out the perfect card, write something loving and encouraging in it, and send it to yourself. Why not make a list of nurturing things, both large and small? Make a list of things you would love to have someone do for you, and do one for yourself each day.

Imagine talking to your best friend and telling him all the wonderful things you've done for yourself. Would that feel comfortable, or would you feel embarrassed? Imagine you are your own best friend, lover, confidant, and caretaker. Allow your life to be something you brag about regularly.

Happiness is not a goal; it is a by-product.

—Eleanor Roosevelt, former first lady

A Walk on the Beach

We all have our own answers. This meditation is an opportunity to relax and connect with the wisdom of your own inner guidance.

Have your journal handy, so you can write down any insights you have after the meditation.

It is a beautiful day. There is a breeze blowing in off the ocean. The air is a bit cool, so you pull your jacket around you. The sand feels cool, soft, and refreshing as you walk along barefoot.

The smell of the sea fills you with a sense of freedom and joy. A short distance offshore, a pod of dolphins frolic and play. You smile as you walk along, thinking, "What a perfect day."

As you walk, you feel at peace, relaxed, and filled with a wonderful, exciting sense of anticipation. An extremely familiar person walks toward you. As they approach, you realize it is your future self. Here is the person you want to become, standing right in front of you.

They embrace you and whisper, "Thank you" in your ear. You look at the person quizzically, and they explain, "It is you who will bring me into being. I am the result of your choices. I can help you if you let me."

You take a deep breath and open yourself up to their guidance and love. As you embrace, you can feel their wisdom, love, and support fill you. You relax, knowing that you already are all you wish you could be. The two of you peacefully walk along the beach, talking and sharing. This truly is a perfect day.

Spend as much time as possible with your future self. Make notes of any insights you have.

The first time I interacted with my future self, I failed to write down my insights. I did the meditation before I went to bed. When I woke up the next morning, I couldn't remember what the insights were, even though they seemed very profound and valuable. I learned the hard way to keep my journal close by when I meditate.

Feeding Your Soul

Try this meditation when you are feeling alone, disconnected, or unloved. It is also very helpful if you aren't feeling well physically.

You are walking along a moss-covered path. It is so soft. It feels wonderful, and you notice how quiet it is walking on it. Off in the distance, the sun reflects off a beautiful white building.

As you approach, you realize it is an ancient temple. Standing in front are two magnificent temple guardians. They have been waiting for you for a very long time. They lovingly welcome you and tell you they've been waiting for you for a long time. They are grateful you have finally come, gently take your hand, and lead you into the temple.

In the center of the room is a skylight. The sun streams down directly onto the pile of pillows. The guardians gently lead you over and gesture for you to lie down. You sink into the pillows and feel totally at peace. The temple feels very familiar, sacred, and loving. You feel surrounded by an expansive healing energy.

You feel someone lovingly place their hand over your heart, and you can feel unconditional love and acceptance pouring into your heart and soul. You hear a voice whispering in your ear, telling you that you are perfect just the way you are.

You feel totally loved, supported, and nurtured. You lay there soaking up the love. You've come home to yourself.

You are grateful you can come back to the temple often and allow it to feed your soul.

Slowly, bringing that sense of connection and love, you bring yourself back to the room.

In this chapter, we explored finding ways to include happiness and joy into your life. You are the most important person in your life.

In the next chapter, you will learn how to make stress a thing of the past.

Part 3

How Else Can I Do That?

As a child I was taught there were two ways of doing things: the right way and the wrong way. There are actually an infinite number of ways to do anything.

The most useful question to ask yourself is: What do I want to create? Do you want to stay with what's familiar and get the same old results, or are you willing to try something new and get the results you really want?

Allowing for the possibility that life is limitless, and that magic and miracles can become everyday events, is a fun way of living life. It is doable and it is simply a matter of being mindful and adjusting your thinking. Anything is possible if you are willing to believe.

Using curiosity and asking yourself, "How else can I do this?" often provides very interesting results. There is the old way of doing things and then an infinite number of other ways.

Experiment, play, and have fun!

Chapter 8

Being Mindful, Releasing Stress

Stress really is optional. The events in your life don't cause the stress; it is the story you tell yourself about the events that cause your upset.

For years I had a profound fear of losing everything, of going bankrupt. Because of that fear, I was miserable a lot of the time. Ironically, I did go bankrupt and lost everything. In the process, I met some wonderful people, moved across the country, and totally changed the way I view life. It was one of the best things that could have happened.

Did I enjoy the experience? NO. I created so much stress and misery for myself, but in hindsight, everything worked out far better than I could have ever imagined. In the process, I became more mindful of my thoughts and changed my filter system. I didn't wake up one day and say, "I think I'll look at how my thoughts create stress." The events in my life certainly invited me to do just that.

You can learn from my drama and consciously choose to examine your filter system. I call it a "filter system" because our beliefs, agreements, attitudes, and assumptions filter what we experience in life. Once you decide to leave stress behind, the quality of life improves dramatically.

By changing the way you view life, everything can become easy. How you think about life can create so much stress and make living so much harder. Change your thoughts, your life, and the world you live in.

Of course, once you begin to realize it's your thoughts that create all your emotional responses to life, change and creating more of what you do want becomes so much easier. When stress, judgment, fear, and limitations are the filters through which you see life, your options are severely limited. You literally can't see the choices that allow life to be easy, joyous, limitless, and fun. Do you want life to be easier and effortless?

Read on, practice using these meditations, become more mindful of your thoughts, and see what happens.

Limitless Living

Yes, there are certain laws of physics, such as gravity, that apply universally. There are others we can suspend by changing our thinking. I used to show people how to walk on fire—to walk on hot, glowing coals without getting burned. You shouldn't be able to do those sorts of things, but you can once you change your beliefs about what's possible. It is amazing how powerful our filter system really is.

I doubt if walking on fire would do much to improve your everyday life. But what about the ability to feel relaxed while sitting in traffic? What if you could feel relaxed even after finding out you have lost your job or your long-term relationship has ended? Those skills could really make a difference.

The word *stress* originally was short for *distress*. It refers to a force or pressure exerted on something. In speech, it refers to the emphasis we place on a word or syllable. Today, it often refers to the pressures of life. *All* stress is induced by your thoughts about events in life and not by life itself. The good news is you can relieve stress by simply changing your thoughts.

There are a couple of tricks for transforming stress, and they work every time if you are willing to let go of your habitual way of thinking.

First, tell yourself a story. The story you habitually tell yourself is not based on fact. Beliefs are only assumptions you have learned to believe about life. Second, consistently ask yourself, "How else can I see this? How can I see this so I feel peaceful, at ease, and safe and know I'm loved? How can I see this through the eyes of love?"

Now I know that going bankrupt was the best thing that could have happened. If I hadn't, I never would have moved across the country to California to study with Don Miguel Ruiz and several other spiritual healers and teachers. Now I own a beautiful home in Hawaii.

The quality of your life is often dependent upon the questions you ask yourself, the answers you give yourself, and the beliefs you create based on your answers. Some answers produce stress and a worldview that is limiting, while others enable you to see a world full of limitless possibilities.

If you do research on stress, you will find these events are the 10 leading causes of stress:

1. Death of spouse
2. Divorce
3. Trying to control external events
4. Moving
5. Death of a close family member
6. Major personal injury or illness
7. Midlife crisis
8. Unemployment
9. Financial worries
10. Retirement

As you review that list, notice what thoughts you have. What are your stories about those events?

I certainly had a lot of opinions about bankruptcy that had very little to do with reality. All emotions are created by what we tell ourselves, even our reactions to death. Our perspectives and our filter systems dictate our experiences. The death of a loved one is certainly a big change, but it doesn't have to be a tragedy; it can be an opportunity to expand your love and remember to be grateful for every moment you have with a loved one.

My mom died in a car accident before I began most of these explorations. I was devastated. My dad died a decade ago. It was an altogether different experience. I held his hand as his spirit left his body. It was a very sacred, peaceful experience.

Floating Down the River

This is a wonderful meditation to use if you are feeling stressed, are concerned about an upcoming event, or just want to relax.

You settle back into a big, comfortable inner tube. It fits your body perfectly. You lean back and relax as you float effortlessly down the river.

The sun filters softly through the canopy of trees overhead. The flickering of the sunlight lulls you gently into a deep state of relaxation. You doze off and on without a care in the world. It feels incredibly freeing to be so relaxed, peaceful, and at ease.

The water is very refreshing. You dip your hands into the water and let it slowly drip off your fingers, watching the ripples it makes.

You lean to one side and notice the inner tube moves effortlessly in that direction. It's fun to direct the inner tube one way and then the other.

Then you begin to notice the light. You travel through areas of bright light, and then you pass into deep shadows. The contrast is very noticeable.

You start thinking about life. You can easily direct your happiness with your thoughts.

If you think in an expansive manner, your happiness expands. If you descend into fear, your life becomes more limited and stress-filled. So, you decide to sit back, relax, and enjoy life.

When you finish the meditation, take some time to write about your thoughts. Use this meditation as an opportunity to be more mindful of your filter system.

> ## Twenty years from now, you will be more disappointed by the things you didn't do than by the ones you did do. So, throw off the bowlines. Sail away from the safe harbor of your old thinking. Catch the trade winds in your sails. Explore. Dream. Discover.
>
> —Mark Twain, writer and humorist

Waves

This is a great meditation to do while stuck in traffic or if you find yourself thinking about something you find upsetting. Generally, when doing these meditations, it is best to do them when you won't be distracted. Some of them, like this one, are a great way to distract yourself and change your habitual thinking.

You are sitting by the shoreline, watching the waves come in and out. The noise from the gently lapping waves is very relaxing. You enjoy watching the patterns the waves make on the sand. You watch as the sand changes color as the water recedes. The shorebirds dart in and out of the waves. The waves curl back onto themselves, rippling and splashing.

As you sit there, you imagine the waves moving inside your body. They fill you with peace and wash away anything unlike peace. As you breathe in, the wave fills you, and as you exhale, the wave washes back out of you.

You sit quietly, feeling the waves wash in and out. You decide to let go of any tiredness, stress, cares, and concerns. You let the waves wash them all away. Then you allow the waves to fill you with peace, love, ease, and joy. You sit, breathing deeply and allowing the waves to work their magic within you and your world.

Letting Order Spread

Years ago, I had a stained-glass studio and plant store. I'd come back from the city with a whole truckload of plants, and after unloading, the store would be a mess and totally chaotic. I had one employee who could gracefully make order out of the mess. One day, I watched in amazement as she cleared a small space on one of the benches, totally ignoring the mess all around her. When I asked her what she was doing, she explained that once she had one spot all neat, clean, and orderly, she just let the beauty spread to the rest of the store. It was incredible to watch!

You can use this meditation to think more clearly or to simply be a neater person.

Turn your eyes upward and to the right while thinking about a small corner of your brain. Imagine it as a room with stacks and stacks of paper everywhere. There are books thrown randomly, scattered on the shelves lining the walls. The curtains on the window are all crooked, and the place is a mess.

In the center, there is a big, comfortable, overstuffed chair. It is your favorite color and looks very inviting. You settle back into the chair, relax, and feel totally at ease. This place is very familiar. You look around and smile. Next to you is a small end table. You take a deep breath, and as you watch, the table is miraculously cleared. It is suddenly neat and orderly. A vase filled with gorgeous flowers appears.

As you glance around the room, you notice that order is beginning to spread. First, one section and then the next miraculously become neatly arranged. You realize that all the information you could ever want or need is available in this room, and you know where it all is.

There is a wonderful fresh breeze blowing. You feel refreshed, at ease, and excited about the limitless possibilities this room contains. You realize you can come back here whenever you want, and you will find your answers. As you sit in the chair, you begin to see life through eyes free of fear, worry, or concerns. You know you are safe, loved, and have all the guidance and assistance you could ever want or need.

It is rumored Mother Teresa had this prayer on her wall:

People are often unreasonable, illogical, and self-centered ...
Forgive them anyway.

If you are kind, people may accuse you of selfish, ulterior motives ...
Be kind anyway.

If you are successful, you will win some false friends and some true enemies ...
Succeed anyway.

If you are honest and frank, people may cheat you ...
Be honest and frank anyway.

If you find serenity and happiness, they may be jealous ...
Be happy anyway.

Give the world the best you have, and it may never be enough ...
Give the world the best you've got anyway.

You see, in the final analysis, it is between you and God;
It was never between you and them anyway.

About Time

Time really isn't linear, even though we often experience it that way. Two of the questions suggested in quantum physics are this: "If we believe we can affect the future by the choices we make today, why do we believe the past is static? If we change the future, why can't we change the past as well?" Actually, we can. Just imagine; it is never too late to have a happy childhood!

Instead of viewing time linearly, we can think of it as ripples in a pond; we can see it as a series of concentric circles. What we place in those circles and how we allow the ripples to affect our lives is up to us, moment by moment, thought by thought.

You have probably had the experience of doing something you find very boring, and time seems to go by very slowly. On the other hand, you've probably been having lots of fun, looked at the clock, and wondered where all the time went. Our perception of time is very fluid and very much dependent upon what we are telling ourselves.

Managing our emotions increases intuition and clarity. It helps us self-regulate our brain chemicals and internal hormones. It gives us natural highs, the real fountain of youth we've been searching for. It enables us to drink from elixirs locked within our cells, just waiting for us to discover them.

—Doc Childre, founder of HeartMath

Bending Time

You really can change your experience of time. If you are worried about being late, see yourself getting there a few minutes early, and relax into the feeling. Every time you get anxious about being late, see yourself easily arriving on time. If you really allow yourself to stay with the feeling of getting there easily and effortlessly and on time, you'll be pleasantly surprised. I have arrived on time when realistically that wasn't physically possible. Time is fluid, and you can be on time even when you should be late. Play with time and see what happens.

You already intuitively know how to speed time up or slow it down. This meditation will give you an opportunity to practice doing it consciously.

Imagine looking at a huge clock and watching the hands slowly moving. Time ticks by very slowly, second by second. The minutes go by leisurely.

Now imagine the hands moving faster and faster. The hands seem to whirl rapidly around and around. The hours speed by. You watch the sun move rapidly through the sky, rising and setting, rising, and setting. Spring turns into summer and summer into fall.

Now imagine the hands slowing down again until they are barely moving. You watch the clock for what seems like hours, and the hands barely move.

Now speed time up again. Take a few long, slow, deep breaths and allow yourself to feel time speeding along. Then take another deep breath and imagine time moving slowly again.

Imagine your clock has a magical button only you can see. You can mentally speed time up or slow it down. When you are in a hurry to get someplace, you can slow time down. You easily get wherever you want to be with plenty of time to spare. Your magic button enables you to use time rather than be used by time. You always have more than enough time for everything.

Spend some time with your journal writing about time. Is time precious? Is relaxing wasting time? What are your beliefs about time?

The conclusion of both modern physics and deep psychology are that things are not what they seem. What we experience as normal reality— about ourselves and nature—is only the tip of an iceberg that arises out of an unfathomable abyss.

—Thomas Moore, author

The Multiplex of Life

It's so easy to begin taking life and ourselves way too seriously. We forget to enjoy each moment and fail to remember what an incredible gift life is, moment by moment.

Imagine you are in the lobby of a huge theater complex. There are hundreds of different movies playing simultaneously. You go to the snack bar, get your favorite snacks, and find the movie featuring you.

You are the star, the producer, the director, the writer, and the filmmaker. You've done it all. You intently watch the first part of the movie. At times, you laugh, cry, get disappointed, and get angry.

After a while, you get tired of the movie. It's boring, it has the same recurring themes and plots, and even though the people change, the characters are the same.

Suddenly you remember you can change movie theaters whenever you want. So, you walk out into the hall, read the marquees, and pick a different movie. You are the star in all of them. Some are comedies, some love stories, there are a few dramas, and one or two are horror films.

You take a deep breath and decide you'd like to see a lighthearted love story for a while. Later you'll try out some of the others. It is very freeing to know you can change your movie at any time.

What's Spirituality Got to Do with It?

Your spirit is the part of you that is eternal, infinite, and immortal. Connecting with your spirit assists you in experiencing the universe as a safe and loving place. When you experience life from the perspective of your mind, it can become overwhelming and scary. Long ago, I heard it said that we are spiritual beings having a physical experience rather than physical beings searching for our spirit.

The word *spirit* originally came from a Latin word that meant "breath." Around 400 c.e. it gradually replaced the word "soul." In many ancient traditions, it is believed that the spirit and breath are one because the spirit connects with the body through the breath.

Spirituality can take on many shapes and forms. It isn't necessarily about God or religion; it's about finding a direct and personal sense of connection. Some people find that connection through religion, but many don't. Spirituality can become a practice that is something you do on a regular basis, such as meditation or yoga, but it doesn't have to be that. Your spiritual connection is your personal connection to the perfection that you really are. It is yours and yours alone. What works for you may not work for anyone else. Spirituality is your personal road map to your divinity.

The Meeting

This meditation will help you connect with your spirit and the sense of inner peace that connection creates.

> You are standing in a beautiful starlight circle. It is a new moon, the time when the moon is dark and the stars are brightest. The wind gently whispers through the trees nearby. You feel at peace and full of love.
>
> A shadow passes overhead, and you feel a deep and abiding connection to something far greater than you. You breathe deeply and allow the magic of the night to fill your heart and your mind.
>
> You hear a voice lovingly calling your name. It tells you, "You are loved, you are loveable, and you are love." You smile as the expansive feeling of unconditional love and acceptance fills each and every cell of your body.
>
> You feel a tender embrace, and you realize you have connected with your spirit. You allow the connection to deepen and grow until you know beyond a doubt that the connection is real.

You open your mind and your heart, knowing you can connect whenever you wish. You realize that incredible wisdom and unconditional love are always just a thought away, and you give thanks.

In this chapter, we explored a variety of ways to become aware of the limitations created by your filter system and ways to transform them. We explored mindfulness and used it to become aware of our filter system and releasing it.

Chapter 9

Wash That Brain

One day, when I was feeling particularly frustrated by my spiritual studies, I complained to one of the other students that a lot of these new concepts seemed like brainwashing. She looked at me very seriously and said, "Your brain *needs* washing." In hindsight, my mind did. It certainly was full of numerous limiting beliefs, agreements, and assumptions.

We are all experts at arguing for our limitations, and we often don't realize that our thoughts create all our limitations.

When was the last time you woke up in the morning, looked in the mirror, and told yourself, "Today, I am going to make myself totally miserable?"

Consciously, you've probably never thought that, yet there have been times that by the end of the day, you have felt miserable. You create misery or happiness and joy thought by thought, choice by choice.

Beliefs Aren't the Truth

I once saw a cartoon of a man and a woman looking into full-length mirrors. The woman was very good-looking, youthful, and thin, yet when she looked at herself, she saw an old, out-of-shape, and overweight woman. The man was balding, had a big beer belly, and was in his 50s. When he looked in the mirror, he saw a young man with long wavy hair, abs of steel, and a muscular build. We see what we believe, then we have an emotional response to that belief. All too often, we make our choices based on those emotions.

If you think your body is ugly, it doesn't really matter what you look like. If you think you need more money in order to be happy, no matter how much money you have, chances are it will never be enough. Changing your external circumstances without changing your beliefs is like trying to sweep the ocean out with a broom. It just isn't very effective.

Beliefs are assumptions about reality that have no concrete proof. Once we believe them, they begin to create limitations.

Up, Up, and Away

You are a limitless being of love and light and laughter. You are totally limitless; your body is your vehicle. Change your beliefs, and your life will change. For a belief to impact your life, you must say it to yourself repeatedly. Beliefs seem like they are second nature, but they are only thoughts.

Most of your beliefs were instilled prior to age seven and were the result of repetitive exposure. Changing a belief merely requires you to repeat the new belief whenever the old belief surfaces and consciously choose to let go of the old one.

This meditation is a wonderful way to symbolically let go of old beliefs.

In front of you, there are a bunch of colorful helium balloons. At the end of each cord, there is a small card. You pick up a pen and begin to write your limiting beliefs on one card after another.

The cards glow, and the ink shimmers. As you finish writing your beliefs, the cards begin to vibrate. With each word, you feel freer and more limitless.

When you are done, you let go of the balloons one by one. You watch as they float higher and higher until you can no longer see them. At your feet, you see a bunch of violet-colored cards. As you read them, you realize they are wonderful replacements for the beliefs you just released.

You read each one slowly, allowing the thoughts to sink in, further erasing the old beliefs, replacing them with a more limitless way of looking at life.

Whenever an old belief surfaces, imagine tying it to a balloon and letting it go.

The Mists of Time

Sometimes we forget how magical life can be. In this meditation, you allow your imagination to get in touch with the limitless possibilities life holds. You really do live in a limitless universe. All limits arise from our beliefs in limitations.

Once you rearrange some of your beliefs, you really can walk on fire. You can consciously begin to create more of what you do want and less of what you don't want.

You stand at the edge of time, a place filled with the energy of creation. It is a place where magic lives and anything is possible.

The swirling mists slowly part, and you watch the birth of stars and galaxies. In the silence, you hear the birth of the universe. The first noises reach you, and they are the sounds of celebration. They are the sounds of the birth of limitless possibilities.

The colors are spectacular. The dancing movements, the endless swirls, the sights, and the sounds are breathtaking.

You watch as the curtain of creation parts, exposing a new universe. The process touches you deeply. You are very much a part of the energy and feel like you are giving birth to yourself.

Creation continues to bubble forth, and suddenly you are aware of yourself as a unique and separate being. You look around and see millions of lights simultaneously spring forth into existence.

You realize you are part of the greater whole. And you give thanks. You stand in the very heart of the universe surrounded by infinite wisdom and unconditional love. You allow yourself to be filled with that love and know you are one.

Take a few moments to fully embrace this experience. Remember, without you, this universe would be incomplete.

Expanding and Contracting

Energy is never static. It is always in motion, either expanding or contracting. Love causes us to expand, while fear causes us to contract. It is important to remember nothing is inherently good or bad. Love isn't better than fear; it is just different. When a semitruck is racing toward you, you can move because you are afraid or because you love yourself. When fear stops you from being vulnerable enough to keep your heart open and love, perhaps you want to make a different choice.

Ultimately, your happiness depends on your choices. You can continue to reaffirm your limiting beliefs, or you can begin making new choices. Your filter system would have you continue making the same old choices and wondering why you keep getting the same results. Your filter system was originally created to make sense of the world, to help you feel safe. It literally filters out anything that challenges its validity.

We tend to judge things as good or bad, right or wrong. We move away from what we don't like instead of consciously choosing to move toward what we do want. When I ask people what they want, I often get a list of what they *don't* want. Focusing on judgments or what we don't want causes us to contract. Whatever we focus our attention on, we get more of, so spend time focusing on what you do want.

Reality is merely an illusion, albeit a very persistent one ... The only thing that interferes with my learning is my education.

—Albert Einstein, physicist

Gratitude is a wonderful way to move beyond judgment and release our limiting beliefs. Gratitude is very expansive. Spend some time each day being grateful for whatever is in your life. Gratitude will also help you release any feelings of separation you might have.

Magical Mirror

Before you do the next visualization, think about something you'd like to change. Take a few moments, think about it, and get a clear image of the problem. Next, get an image of how you would like to feel or act. What do you want to create? For example, if you tend to get stressed in traffic or before a business meeting or a date, create a mental picture of yourself feeling stressed. Next, picture what it would look like to feel totally at ease, relaxed, and confident.

You can use this meditation to change just about anything, including long-standing habits. Next time you are in the middle of a strong emotional reaction, use it to center yourself. If you want to use this to quit smoking or shed extra weight, then every time you feel like smoking or are about to eat, use this visualization.

You walk into a room that shimmers with an amazing feeling of magic and miracles.

It contains a large, magical mirror. You go and stand in front of the mirror with a luminescent blue frame.

You see yourself clearly in the mirror feeling overwhelmed and stressed, experiencing an unwanted behavior or feeling.

You stand watching the image for a moment, and then you take a long, slow, deep breath. As you exhale, you see the image of what you do want off in the distance. It's racing toward the back of the blue-framed mirror.

It smashes through the mirror, breaking the unwanted behavior into millions of tiny pieces. The limiting behavior immediately dissolves into nothingness.

The image of what you do want gets bigger and bigger. The image appears before you in a mirror. The mirror now has a white frame that glows with a magical hum.

You take another deep breath and allow yourself to be filled with the image of what you want to create.

Practice switching between the two images, and focus on the outcome each choice creates. Make sure there is a big difference emotionally. Make the wanted behavior very emotionally rich and highly desirable. Let the desired behavior easily replace the old unwanted behavior.

I used to smoke three packs of cigarettes a day. Over 30 years ago, I stopped smoking permanently by using a similar visualization.

I created two very clear, distinct images to visualize during the moments when I really wanted to smoke again. In one, I chose to take a cigarette out and smoked it, but then I had to smoke a whole tractor-trailer load of cigarettes. In the other image, I chose not to smoke. I was free of the addiction and smelled good, my breathing was better, and I experienced an immense feeling of freedom.

I made that choice repeatedly whenever the urge to smoke popped up. I have used that trick anytime I struggle with changing anything, and so can you.

Clouds

Clouds come in all different shapes and forms. They look substantial, yet if you try to hold on to one, there isn't anything solid about them. They are as amorphous as our thoughts. This meditation helps you allow your thoughts to have less impact and makes changing the way you think a bit easier.

It is a wonderful practice, either real or imagined. As the saying goes, if you're too busy to take a few minutes for yourself, you are *too* busy. Make a point of looking around and noticing nature and the people around you.

Imagine lying on your back, looking up at the sky, and watching the clouds as they float effortlessly by. They move seamlessly. Some grow larger while others simply fade away.

As you look at the clouds, you begin to see shapes and forms, lions and tigers and bears and angels and planes. The images are only limited by your imagination.

You watch as the shadows of the clouds move over the land. You notice how they move effortlessly. There is no resistance or struggle, just easy and endless motion.

You begin to visualize your thoughts as clouds moving over your mental landscape. Your thoughts don't have to be any more solid than clouds. You can let them effortlessly drift along, without reacting or resisting them. Your thoughts can only affect you if you let them.

You can just watch your thoughts float by, choose to believe them, or to focus your attention on love, acceptance, and joy.

You choose to focus your attention on thoughts that create freedom and joy. You let limiting thoughts float effortlessly and endlessly by.

Did you ever watch clouds as a child? My mom and I used to play a game, naming the clouds. Decide to take a moment and notice your surroundings; this is the only time you can experience this moment. Embrace each moment fully and savor the moment.

Somewhere, something incredible is waiting to be known.

—Carl Sagan, astronomer and writer

Assumptions

Assumption is an interesting word. It means being taken into heaven as well as arrogant and pretentious. When you make an assumption and don't specifically share it with others, there is frequently a disagreement afterward. Assumptions are always based on our filter systems, and each of us sees the world from our own unique perspective.

One of my first students was a man named Mark. He had AIDS long before there was any treatment for it. Most people think having a disease is a "bad" thing. Health is good, and disease is bad. Disease means we need to heal something. The author Louise Hay saw disease as a call for love. Mark and I had long conversations about love and about accepting *whatever is present* in our lives. He never fought AIDS; he accepted it and lived fully with it. Mark got a great job, bought a home, went to school, and enjoyed every moment of his life. He chose to live passionately for five years, and the moment he died, he no longer had AIDS.

I watched other friends fight the disease valiantly. Their lives were consumed with finding new treatments and trying to overcome society's prejudice. All noble pursuits, but they died without ever fully savoring and enjoying living. (Of course, now there are many treatments for HIV. Mark made the best choice available in the early 1980s.)

Life is a fatal disease. We all die. The question is what we will do with the time between our birth and our death. Will we live passionately, savoring every moment and being fully alive, or will we resist life and die before we really live?

Wholeness and Holiness

You are already perfect just the way you are, and so is the world around you. Connecting with that perfection unleashes the incredible power of your innate holiness, wisdom, and grace.

If you decide to live from that perfection, life becomes a magical experience of wonder and joy. Living from that connection takes practice, but it is well worth the effort.

Set aside ten or twenty minutes where you will be free of distractions, and no one will disturb you. Then just relax into this meditation.

Play with the idea of perfection. Imagine perfection as a state of being rather than an external measurement.

Imagine a bubble of perfection surrounding you and filling you with a deep sense peace, relaxation, and ease. That bubble erases any judgments or doubts.

As you breathe in, the bubble grows. As you exhale, any judgments just blow away and dissolve. That feeling of perfection fills each and every cell of your being.

Like an ice cube placed in a hot cup of tea, you feel your consciousness melted by the energy of perfection.

You surrender all thoughts and feelings to this bubble of perfection, and you give thanks.

You breathe in that expansive feeling of oneness, connection, and freedom. You breathe out anything unlike perfection.

As you connect with that, knowing that you are perfect, you allow yourself to connect with your wholeness and your holiness. You are perfect just the way you are.

You always have been, and you always will be. Allow that knowing to fill your entire being.

The state of your life is nothing more than a reflection of your state of mind.

—Dr. Wayne W. Dyer, author and inspirational speaker

Everything Is Relative

When it comes to concepts, spirituality, and philosophy, there is no such thing as *the truth*. The truth is relative and changes over time.

As a species, we seem so much more comfortable when we think we know the truth and when most people agree with our version. Many years ago, people believed the world was flat, and people who disagreed were put to death for heresy.

As soon as we believe something is true, we close our minds to other possibilities. Our belief in the truth severely limits our experience of reality.

You can be comforted by your beliefs and still allow for the possibility that there is a more expansive way of looking at life. Curiosity is one of the greatest gifts and most powerful tools you have. Be curious about everything. The quality of your life is often dependent on the quality of the questions you ask yourself.

When you are having a strong emotional reaction to something, remember you have a choice. Take a deep breath and ask yourself the following questions:

- Is this the way I want to feel?
- How else could I think about this?
- Do I want to be right or happy?
- How can I see this through the eyes of love?
- What beliefs do I have about this?
- Am I choosing how to act, or am I reacting?

Brain Washing

This meditation can be rather humorous, and it is very powerful. A sense of humor can make life and change easier and more enjoyable.

You find yourself standing in front of a cosmic washing machine. You add soap to the washer, place belief softener in the softener dispenser, and set the water temperature to warm. You listen to the water as it gently fills the machine.

You take a deep breath, place your hands on either side of your head, and remove your brain. For a few moments, you watch as the machine agitates your brain. The water looks pretty murky, so you add a little more soap.

After the first cycle, you take out your brain, and it still looks a bit dirty, so you wash it again. You watch the rinse water and see all those limiting beliefs washing away. You feel so much freer as the washer spins your brain dry, removing the last bits of limiting thinking.

You remove your brain from the washer, and it smells fresh and clean. It feels lighter. You try it on, and you are immediately filled with joy and laughter. You feel free and wonder why it took you so long to wash your brain. You vow to wash it again if any of those limiting old thoughts return.

In this chapter, we explored the power of beliefs and saw them for what they really are (limiting filters created by assumptions). Now you have a variety of ways to change them.

As you release judgments, you can begin to connect with the essence of who and what you are and begin to feel the perfection of life, of yourself, and about what is.

Chapter 10

Tune-Ups

Our bodies are incredible. Bones can break, and the body rebuilds them even stronger than before. With little or no care, our bodies can last for decades; if we nurture and care for them, who knows how long they can last?

Your body is your vehicle; it is the way you move through physical reality. You can view it as a sacred temple that houses your spirit and treat it accordingly.

When your mind, body, and spirit are working together to create a loving experience, miracles happen.

Because you are a mind, body, spirit trinity housed in your body, it makes sense to approach health from a holistic perspective.

Energy in Motion

Our bodies mirror our beliefs, agreements, attitudes, and assumptions. We each carry all our thoughts someplace in our bodies. Emotions are energy in motion. When we don't allow them to flow freely, we hold them in our bodies. Our bodies change when we let go of our anger, fear, and sadness and instead fill ourselves with joy, health, and abundance.

When I lived in San Diego, I would go to the beach every day, sit on my beach chair, and write in my journal. Then I would meditate and imagine the wind blowing through me, releasing anything that no longer served me and filling my body with love and joy.

Remember, your beliefs aren't real. Allow for the possibility that your body is profoundly affected by your thoughts. You can change your life, your thoughts, and in the process, your body. When you notice yourself judging your body, send it love instead. When you feel the discomfort of pain, use one of these visualizations to release it. Listen to your body, follow your inner wisdom, and watch your life blossom.

Your thoughts have a profound effect on your body, your life, and your daily choices.

The power of love to change bodies is legendary, built into folklore, common sense, and everyday experience. Love moves the flesh; it pushes matter around .... Throughout history, "tender loving care" has uniformly been recognized as a valuable element in healing.

—Larry Dossey, physician

Scanning Your Body

With a bit of practice, scanning your body can become second nature. Love really does have the power to heal. The first step in maintaining a healthy body starts with being in touch with what your body needs.

This meditation will help you have more awareness of your body and its needs.

As always, find a comfortable spot where you won't be disturbed.

Take a few deep breaths and gently close your eyes. When you open your eyes, you see a large, beautiful, colorful flat screen monitor. You touch your head, and you see energy buzzing around. You realize you are seeing a projection of your body on the screen.

In front of you is a console with buttons and a variety of colored lights.

Starting at the top of your head, you see a variety of different colors. You move the pointer and explore your scalp, head, face, ears, and brain. You see and feel energy.

When you notice any place there might be some tension, you let it go by filling that area with a brilliant pink and white light.

You use the pointer to start at your head and slowly go through your entire body. The area around your shoulders and back is a murky color, so you spend more time filling that area with the white light.

Next, you scan your torso and go inside, exploring each of your organs, sending them light, until they feel energized.

You notice your stomach, inside and out, lighting up your pelvis, hips, and buttocks with the healing balm of love. You slowly let the energy glide down your legs and allow the light to focus on your knees, ankles, and feet.

You fill up each cell and every molecule of your body, filling them with love.

If you notice any discomfort, the monitor asks it what it needs. You really listen to your body. By the time you are done, you know if it needs more rest, water, or exercise

Does your body need more broccoli or some chocolate?

What exactly does your body need?

Take a few minutes to write down any insights, thoughts, or suggestions you get during the meditation.

Taking 15-second mini-breaks during the day is a wonderful way to care for your body. Pause frequently, stop what you are doing, and take a long, slow, mindful breath. When you exhale, let everything go. It only takes one deep breath to change the way you are feeling.

Playing with Pain

Pain is your body's way of letting you know something is going on. You don't have to suffer with pain; you can learn to use it to get more information about what is happening in your body and learn to turn the volume down on the pain. You can practice this meditation anytime, but it is easier if you practice using it when you are just having a minor ache or pain. If you try this meditation for the first time when you are in severe pain, it is easy to get lost. The likelihood of success is diminished.

With a little practice, you can successfully control your pain. I have taught many people to use this meditation to get rid of aches, pains, headaches, and severe menstrual cramps. It is amazing how changing the size, shape, and color of pain can make such a difference.

Simply allow yourself to be with your pain. You once again see your body up on the screen. As you observe your body up on the screen, you breathe into the pain until you are just aware of it, without fear or judgment. Just be with the pain.

You notice if the pain has a color, what color would it be?

Use the console to play with the color. Make it brighter and darker, solid or more transparent. Notice what happens to the pain. Does the pain lessen or increase as you play with the color and the density?

What shape would it be? Does it have rough edges, or is it smooth? Make it larger or smaller and notice what happens to the pain. Imagine the pain has a small mouth and ask it what message it has for you. Talk lovingly to it and listen. Ask it what it needs and how you can be of service.

Once you are done, you can adjust the color and the size until you no longer have any discomfort and the pain is gone. You can use this meditation during childbirth, although there will be a meditation specifically designed for that later in the chapter.

Oh, My Aching Head

I had migraines for years. I would get nauseous and found it necessary to avoid light by sitting in a darkened room. Even the slightest noise was extremely painful. I began to fear the onset of a migraine.

Once I began meditating, my symptoms diminished. This visualization banished migraines from my life. On the extremely rare occasion I feel one starting, this meditation gets rid of it immediately. It is also great for simple tension headaches.

Imagine yourself walking down a flight of stairs that lead to the very center of your being.

As you walk down the stairs toward the core of your being, you are aware of the pain in your head. Off in the background, you become aware of the beating of a drum.

As you approach your center, you become aware of the incredibly brilliant light of unconditional love. You allow it to infuse every cell of your body. The drumbeat fades into the background, filling you with a sense of love, connection, peace, and ease.

You rest in the love, surrender to the light, and allow yourself to relax into it. The beating of the drum becomes a distant echo. You spend time bathing in the light of love. You let that light fill you as it soothes your entire being.

When you feel ready, you begin to slowly ascend the stairs and return to normal waking consciousness. You gladly leave the discomfort behind. Step by step, you become more alive, feeling totally at peace, grateful the discomfort is no longer with you. The drum becomes the loving, nurturing beating of your heart.

Some people find it necessary to do this meditation several times before their headache completely disappears.

It's important to notice the change between the pain on the way down and the diminishing discomfort on the way back up. Remember to leave the pain behind.

> ## Try not. Do, or don't do. There is no try.
> —Yoda, from the movie Star Wars

You Are Getting Sleepy ...

Millions of people suffer from insomnia. Many people are so busy. They put themselves last on their to-do list and are often sleep-deprived as a result. Getting a good night's rest can make an incredible difference in your life. If you are too busy to take care of yourself, you are too busy, period! Creating a regular sleep routine helps as well. Make it simple and do the routine mindfully, with the intent of falling asleep easily and effortlessly.

With this meditation, I seldom make it past 93 before I drift off.

Get as comfortable as possible. Take a long, slow, deep breath. Mentally give yourself permission to relax and let go. Imagine a large basket right outside your front door. One by one, you place all your cares and concerns in the basket. You know that they will disappear, get taken care of, or be there waiting for you in the morning. You take a long, slow, deep breath and really let go.

See yourself standing in front of a large blackboard. You pick up the chalk, and on the left side of the board, you write 100 in large, graceful numbers. Now on the right side, you write, "I am falling asleep." Erase the board and write 99 on the left side and "I am falling asleep" on the right side. Again, erase the board and write 98 and "I am falling asleep."

Continue counting backward until you fall asleep.

Vibrantly Alive

Your body can heal itself once you get out of the way. Visualizing is a wonderful way to nurture, regenerate, and heal the body.

Here are some simple suggestions for using your mind to work with your body:

- Dealing with pain: Acknowledge it with love and think of it as an opportunity to heal. Ask your body what it needs, and then listen for the answer.
- Aging: Instead of thinking, "I am getting old," think of your body being filled with wisdom and grace.
- Body-size issues: Stand naked in front of a mirror and release any judgments you have. Consciously choose to send love to each part of your body, give thanks for it, and realize it is perfect just the way it is.
- Strong emotions: Pretend you are blowing out a candle and blow out the emotion, consciously letting it go with each breath. When you are finished releasing the emotions, inhale love and self-acceptance.
- Illness: There is nothing inherently wrong with being sick. It might not feel good, but it isn't a bad thing either. Embrace whatever is going on in your body, view it as an invitation to love yourself more deeply, and then listen to what your body is telling you.

No matter what the question or the problem, love is always the answer.

Feeling Fine

At the end of a hypnosis session, I will say, "In a moment, you will be wide awake, feeling fine and in perfect health, much better than before."

Your brain is constantly sending messages to your body. What do you think about your body? Do you love it or judge it? This meditation will help you send your body the kind of messages you want it to receive and that would be most useful to your life and body.

Take some time getting comfortable. Turn off your phone and allow yourself to relax.

You are gently walking through a beautiful garden. The path is covered with moss and feels very soft underfoot. The air is rich and clean and fresh. There is a gentle breeze that lovingly caresses you. You feel totally at peace and at ease.

As you round the corner, you see a fountain of light. It shimmers. Rainbows of light dance in endless patterns. The light show fascinates you; a feeling of peace and profound relaxation enfolds you.

You walk over to the fountain, watch for a moment longer, and then you smile and step into the center. You feel the light washing through you. You feel joy bubbling up through the soles of your feet.

Your body gets lighter and freer and filled with love. Any judgments or limiting thoughts about your body wash effortlessly away. You feel incredibly free.

Suddenly, images of the perfection of your body begin to flow through your mind. You are filled with gratitude for your body. You realize it is a wonderful gift. You see it as the perfect vehicle for your spirit.

You give thanks and allow your body to be filled with that sense of gratitude. You take a deep breath and allow light to wash through you. It washes through every cell and molecule, filling them with vibrant health.

Your body begins to vibrate with all the colors of the rainbow. The colors wash away any stress, cares, concerns, or discomfort. Your body feels better than it ever has before.

You stand in the center of that fountain for as long as you wish. When you step out of the fountain, your body is brand new, vibrantly alive, and completely at ease.

This is a great visualization to use when you are standing in line, stopped in traffic, or just trying to relax.

Scrubbing Bubbles

Your body's white cells are amazing little creatures. This meditation helps you create wonderful mental pictures, ones you can use to harness your body's ability to heal itself. This is a great meditation to do at the end of your day

Take a deep breath and focus your full attention on your body. Slowly, your body begins to relax and shimmer with light. You see a projection of your body on a translucent screen directly in front of you. You see hundreds and hundreds of tiny scrubbing bubbles circulating through your body. They move effortlessly and easily through your body, cleaning, healing, and renewing every cell.

They flow through all your blood vessels, cleaning the walls and carrying oxygen to your entire body. They zoom through your organs, removing any debris or unnecessary build-ups. They make everything in your body shiny and brand new.

Behind them, there are tiny maintenance workers repairing and replacing anything that is the slightest bit worn. They straighten everything up, build new cells, and make your body flexible and fluid. They fill you with a sense of ease and vibrancy. You smile as you watch them rushing through your body. No task is too big or too small. They return your body to optimum health. You feel refreshed. You feel great. And you give thanks.

Take a few minutes to just sit, be with the energy, and allow it to sink in. Allow yourself to really savor the process. Whenever you feel any discomfort in your body, view it as a call to action. Send in the maintenance workers!

Miracles happen, not in opposition to nature but in opposition to what we know of nature.

—Saint Augustine, theologian and philosopher

Why Wait?

If you wait for your happiness until you change something or until tomorrow, it will never get here because by the time tomorrow gets here, it's today. If you'll be happy when you lose some weight or have more muscle mass, you are giving away your opportunity to be happy right now. Your best bet is to be happy about what you *do* have and then take actions consistent with what you want to create.

You can use your mind to help you change your body but only if you are willing to stop judging where you are. Remember from Chapter 6 how judgment acts like cosmic superglue? Take time to visualize your perfection now!

> Imagine standing in front of a magical mirror. As you look into it, you see your body exactly how you would like it to be. You turn and look at your body from every angle, and it is absolutely perfect.
>
> You see and feel its perfection. You look at yourself in that mirror, and you are absolutely amazed at how great you look. You are so happy you find yourself doing a happy dance.
>
> You take one step forward and step directly into the image you see in the mirror. You fit perfectly into your new body.
>
> You slowly feel every inch of your body. Yes, it is real, and it is perfect, and it is yours. You take a deep breath and give thanks.
>
> Every time you think of your body, choose what to eat, or decide whether to exercise, think of that image. Take a deep breath, become that body, and then make your choice.

A bodily disease, which we look upon as whole and entire within itself, may, after all, be but a symptom of some ailment in the spiritual part.

—Nathaniel Hawthorne, novelist and short-story writer

Giving Birth

Moment by moment, we give birth to our lives, to ourselves, and all aspects of our lives.

Some women also have the good fortune to give birth to a child. The following meditation is a great way to give birth to yourself, and it is also a useful meditation to use before giving birth to your child.

You hear the rustling of angels' wings and the celebration of a life about to begin. Deep within the womb, the tiny body moves; it is about to be born, and it is excited about beginning a new life. A feeling of peace and ease settle around mother and child. They are both filled with the remembrance of the joy life brings. The remembrance of the concepts that ease and effortlessness bring to life, and you allow them to flow through the air around you.

There is the sound of water rushing, and the journey begins. The room is filled with the love and light and laughter of spirit. As the birth unfolds, both mother and child are infused with that love. That love eases the pain and makes the process one of celebration rather than labor.

The baby takes their first breath, and all the beings of light surround the newborn, welcoming the young spirit and enfolding the baby with love. They all whisper, "You are loved, you are lovable, and you are love. You are now and will always be connected. We are only a thought away, we love you, and we will always be here for you."

You imagine remembering your own birth and smile. They were there for you as well and still are. You mentally reach out and feel the loving support of the beings that surround you, the ones always filled with love and light and laughter.

In this chapter, you learned how to get rid of some types of pain, sleep better, and use your mind as a tool for healing. You met your magical maintenance workers and set them loose in your body.

Chapter 11

Play Nice

Life is just a series of relationships. There are our relationships with the world, our families, ourselves, our bodies, money, time, love, and our beliefs about life. The list goes on and on. Once we master the art of relationships, life becomes a much more joyous adventure.

It really doesn't matter what you are dealing with; the basic skills are all the same.

One of the most useful questions you can explore at any given moment is, "Right now, do I want to be right, or do I want to be happy?" Whenever you are having any sort of conflict, these questions are mutually exclusive.

Finding the Similarities

I am you, you are me, and we are one. When you view life from that perspective, intimacy and joy increase exponentially.

When you feel like it is "them" out there and you over here, loneliness and anger grow as well. Intimacy deepens if you consciously choose to search for the common denominator in all your relationships.

You also can see that the problem and solution are one and the same.

What do you really want to get out of your relationships, and what are you willing to give? You can steadfastly see things your way or choose to see life through the eyes of love instead.

Dance of Life

When I moved to the Big Island of Hawaii, my Hawaiian *kumu* (teacher) took me to hula classes. At first, I tried to dance by learning the movements. It wasn't much fun, and it was hard.

As I connected with the spiritual aspects of the dance, it took on a totally new meaning. I was no longer attempting to learn a series of dance movements. Instead, it became a wonderful way for me to connect with my spirit. I began to enjoy the process immensely.

Life can be a series of events or a process in which you connect with who and what you really are. As you learn to approach all of life with curiosity, you can enjoy the process, no matter what.

And as we let our own light shine, we unconsciously give other people permission to do the same. As we are liberated from our fear, our presence automatically liberates others.

—Marianne Williamson, author and lecturer

This is a meditation that will help you expand your perspective and embrace the essence of who and what you really are.

Take some time to relax, get comfortable, and then let your imagination take you to this ancient forest. Engage your senses, feel the air, smell the forest, and surrender to the experience. Let your body sink into the experience.

You are in the center of a beautiful clearing in an ancient forest. You close your eyes, and your body slowly begins to move rhythmically.

The full moon is directly overhead, and its light magically dances with you. You freely listen to the mystical rhythm emanating from deep within your heart.

Your body moves easily and effortlessly. You are amazed at the fluidity, grace, and joy with which your body moves. You realize you aren't moving your body mentally; you are simply allowing your body to move to the tempo of your spirit.

As you breathe in, you breathe in peace, joy, and ease. When you breathe out, you let go of all thoughts of struggle, control, or "I can't do this."

You surrender fully and completely to your spirit and allow yourself to dance. You feel the rhythm of your heart, the gentle cadence of your spirit, and you allow it to flow through you.

You feel the magic that is you. You realize you can fight life or surrender to the flow. You joyously surrender to the dance of life and know ease.

Just imagine yourself in the clearing, embraced by the moonlight, and dancing in celebration of life.

You feel the magic that is you, and it feels wonderful.

Curiosity

Have you ever watched a child explore something, their face full of wonder, totally in the moment, filled with curiosity, and in awe of life?

When you approach life with that kind of curiosity, the results are often far better than when we think we already know.

Set the stage for this meditation. You could light a candle, play music, and just relax into the experience of being in space. You are living on a planet that moves through space. You have been on spaceship earth all your life. So, expand your thoughts, use your imagination, and relax into this meditation.

Take a long, slow, deep breath and brace yourself. You are about to open the hatch on your spaceship.

This is your first day on a brand-new planet. You've been told that the planet is totally safe and very sensual. You have a day to explore the area and have as many experiences as possible. You aren't exactly sure what to expect, but you are excited and know it will be wonderful.

You walk out of the spaceship and smell the air. It smells wonderful. You are filled with a sense of excitement, wonder, and joy.

You feel so lucky to have this opportunity. You throw caution to the wind and begin to run through the gardens, laughing, and shouting at the top of your lungs. You feel so safe, alive, and free.

Everything looks so different. There are colors, shapes, and smells you have never experienced before. You feel like a little child filled with curiosity. You aren't sure which is more exciting, the new sights and sounds or the feeling of curiosity.

You surrender to the feeling of curiosity. As you dive into curiosity, you notice how expansive and free you feel. You realize this world is totally limitless, and yours can be, too, if you unleash your curiosity. What a gift curiosity is!

You notice how being curious feels in your body. Your skin feels so alive. Your body feels like it is vibrating. Everything looks so much more alive.

Curiosity feels so expansive. You are so grateful you have allowed yourself to embrace it. Your imagination soars, and you allow your curiosity to set you free.

Take some time to explore, really explore and embrace this experience. What would your life be like if you approached your thinking and life with curiosity?

Giving 100 Percent

There is a big difference between trying to get something by giving and having an open heart and giving to simply share love. The first is manipulation and not really giving at all. We can give without expecting anything in return, but it takes willingness and practice. Being honest enough to know the difference between the two is very freeing and an asset in improving the quality of our relationships.

Unfortunately, many relationships are often unnegotiated trade agreements. If you do this, I'll love you, and I want you to do this in return. So often, love isn't love at all. It is conditional, and it is really fear dressed up in a costume. Learning to know the difference and only offer real love makes a huge difference in our lives and in the people, events, and outcomes we attract.

Why not light a candle or some incense? Set the stage for a sacred, loving moment.

Imagine you are sitting quietly, feeling connected to the greater whole. You are filled with love, and that feeling flows toward everyone and everything.

You breathe in love and acceptance and breathe out anything unlike love and acceptance. The bubble of love and acceptance surrounding you shimmers.

You allow yourself to be with that feeling and imagine what it is like to have an open heart, free of fear. You imagine what it would feel like to be able to give 100 percent of yourself without the fear of being taken advantage of.

Just breathe in that feeling until you feel ready.

Now imagine someone you've had a difficult time dealing with is sitting across from you. He is also immersed in that bubble of love and acceptance.

Feel the love flowing into you, through your heart, and going toward him like a beam of light. Imagine him judging you, and see the ribbon of love continuing to flow through you and into him.

See him acting in a way you considered judgmental or unloving. Continue to let the love flow toward him. Feel what it feels like to love 100 percent of the time.

For a moment, allow yourself to slip back into judging him. Feel the love stopping; you no longer allow it to flow. Think about being right, judge his actions, and feel self-righteously angry about how he speaks to you. Notice what happens to you and how you feel when you stop the love. How does it feel to judge and be right?

Consciously choose to let the love flow outward again. Let go of your judgments. Accept whatever is and feel the love as it fills you with peace, joy, and laughter.

Give, just for the pure joy of giving and not with the expectation that he will be kind or loving in return. Love, just love. Notice how much better it feels.

Take a deep breath and come back from the meditation. In any given moment, you have a choice of love or judgment and fear. Which feels better to you? When has judgment or fear created exactly what you want in your life?

Practice choosing love. When you feel a judgment rise to the surface, consciously let it go, love yourself, the judgment, and the object you feel like using as an excuse to let go of the love. Then choose again, choose love.

Where Does Their Part Begin?

When we choose to find fault, happiness remains elusive. Statements like "You hurt my feelings" or "You made me mad" do nothing to improve the quality of your life or your relationships. Those statements are inaccurate. The truth is what you tell yourself about what happened is what generates your anger and hurts your feelings.

You can make a huge difference by going within and seeing what really upset you, sharing that with the intent of getting closer, and listening— really listening—to what the other person says.

Next time you get in a disagreement with someone, listen to yourself. Do you want to be right or happy? Remember your emotions. Yes, each of your emotions is generated by what you tell yourself. If you choose to see the world and everyone in it as perfect, your ability to love increases, as does your sense of freedom and your feelings of joy.

I have found that gratitude helps erase judgments and helps us see life through the eyes of love. Find a blank greeting card (or make one). On the cover, write "Thank You." Then inside, list all the things you are grateful for having. List everything, even things like soft toilet paper.

If there is something you want to have, write that on a slip of paper. Spend a few minutes every night reading your gratitude list, being grateful for everything you have, and seeing yourself already having the thing you want. Feel it and see it already existing in your life—right here, right now.

Being Mindful Sets You Free

We tend to live our lives on autopilot. When you are mindful, you can make conscious choices on what to think. Instead of reacting to life, you can make choices. Our emotions are reactions to our old, often limiting beliefs. How often have you thought, "That person really makes me angry?"

Deciding to be mindful allows you to choose your emotional responses to life. Being mindful helps us create the life of our dreams.

Have you ever sincerely wanted something and realized it didn't feel as good as you thought it would when you got it?

Questions are the path to mindfulness. Instead of allowing your mind to run amuck, begin to deepen your awareness of your filter system.

What are my beliefs, agreements, assumptions, and attitudes? Do you see life through the eyes of love? How expansive is your definition of love?

Is being right, affirming your version of reality, important? How do you define happiness?

Decide, just for a day, to be really mindful of your thoughts. How often do you get distracted, and what distracts you?

Letting Go of Limits

Boundaries are a funny thing. We can use them to enhance or limit our intimacy or our ability to get close. It all depends on what we really want to create.

Knowing whether we really wanted to get closer is often much clearer in hindsight. We all need to be able to set boundaries and know what we want and need. The irony is that once we get comfortable setting boundaries, we don't need to set them very often.

Imagine finding yourself floating in the darkness of space, high above Earth. The globe, as it floats below you, is breathtaking.

The oceans and clouds are vibrantly alive. As you drift effortlessly overhead, you watch the division between light and dark move around Earth. You are filled with a sense of wonder and awe.

The continents stand out sharply against the oceans. From space, it looks like a pristine place, but you know the land is full of people, and the oceans teem with life.

You blink and find yourself sitting on a chair, looking at a globe spinning slowly on its axis. The boundaries between the various countries catch your attention, and you notice how divided the continents look. You think about all the wars that have been fought to protect those boundaries. When there are no boundaries, Earth is all one. When seen from that perspective, Earth looks so fragmented.

Next, you find yourself in a large city, standing on a street corner, surrounded by cars and people. There is a sense of chaos, but you choose to focus on the celebration of life. There is so much life on this small planet called Earth.

You take a deep breath, and you are again in space seeing Earth below you in all its glory. The greens and blues are incredibly vivid. The land and the oceans teem with life. You have moved beyond the illusion of boundaries and of separation. From this perspective, you can see the oneness.

You think about your life and the limitless possibilities that lie just beyond the boundaries created by your filter system. You take a deep breath and let them all go. You connect with the essence of who and what you are and know what you want and need without those artificial boundaries.

You are perfect, whole, and complete, and you make all your choices from that sense of oneness.

What Did You Say?

Did you ever play that game of telephone when you were a kid? The first person whispers something to the person sitting next to them, and everyone passes on what they heard. When the last person tells everyone what they heard, it is often very different from what was originally said. Not clearly hearing what is said and assuming you know what was said has caused more than one relationship to end.

This meditation helps you learn to really listen to yourself and to others.

In front of you is a huge box full of toys. You smile as you sort through it. You are reminded of many wonderful and long-forgotten memories.

At the bottom of the box, you find a magical megaphone and headset. They enable you to clearly hear what is being said and assist everyone in hearing what you are saying. It magically translates words, so all your communications are crystal clear.

Your words and your thoughts are free of the limitations created by your filter system's version of reality.

As you play with the megaphone and headset, you are amazed at how differently you hear what people say.

You practice frequently until listening clearly, and ignoring your filter system becomes second nature. You listen to the sounds around you and the beating of your heart. Your hearing is more sensitive than ever before. You practice listening to your friends and family, and you hear not just the words, but you also hear the essence of what they are truly saying.

As you breathe and relax into the experience, you realize using the megaphone and headset becomes a choice you can easily make anytime and anyplace.

All you need to do is take a deep breath and listen—really listen. Listening is a choice. You can choose to hear what you think people are saying or really listen to what they are actually saying.

You now know you have the choice, and you practice listening with your heart and entire being. You listen and give thanks for the opportunity to hear.

Fear-Based Love or Love-Based Love?

When our love is conditional, it is fear-based. When our love is free of judgments or conditions, it is love-based. Loving unconditionally is something we can aspire to achieve. Part of the human condition is to put conditions on our love. Acknowledging that our love is conditional enables us to release some of the fear and love more openly and passionately.

Love comes from a Latin word meaning "to please." One of several definitions for love is having an unselfish, loyal, and benevolent concern for the good of another. In real life, love is often not about that.

Take some time to look at your definition of love. Not what you assume love is or the fear-based love so prevalent in our reality.

Falling in and out of love is only possible when that love is conditional or fear-based love. It isn't really love at all when my actions say, "I'll love you as long as you are nice to me and act according to my rules, but if you don't, I will withdraw my love."

A lot of what we call love is really just an unspoken trade agreement we never negotiated verbally, "I'll do this if you do that."

The Mystery of Love

The emotion of love is a very powerful chemical force in our body and affects our lives in a profound manner. How you use love is up to you. You can use this meditation to expand your definition and experience of love. (You'll read a lot more about love in Chapter 12.)

It is a beautiful summer morning. You have no place you must be, and you feel totally at peace and relaxed. The air has the promise of a warm day to come, but it is fresh, clean, and cool.

You sit and watch as the sun slowly embraces the garden before you. The roses are in full bloom, they smell sweet, and the dew encases the blossoms. It is heavenly to just sit and allow the start of a new day to unfold gently.

You breathe in the sweet smell of summer and are incredibly grateful to be alive. As you watch a butterfly flit by and a hummingbird feed from a nearby flower, you are filled with a sense of love. You think about the mystery of love, all the words written about love, the ups, the downs, and the magic of it all.

You hear a buzzing near your ear. When you turn to look, you notice a small angel flying around you. She tells you she is here to teach you about love. She flies around your heart, and you feel warmth filling your entire being. You are suddenly flooded with feelings of love, acceptance, and joy. It feels so good to be filled with unconditional, expansive love.

The angel lovingly explains your filter system and how it distorts your experience and limits your ability to make other choices. You see a new world, expansive, full of freedom and joy, based on love.

She offers to tell you love's secrets, and you listen intently to every word she has to say. As you listen, you feel that deep sense of love expanding and growing. The idea of love, free of judgments and limits, fills you.

You begin to understand love. Her words touch you deeply, and you know your understanding will continue to blossom and grow. Your ability to love, to just love, washes away all your judgments and fear. You know you can shine the light of love on your thoughts and watch them magically transform. You know you're able to love deeply and completely.

You are so grateful for her love, guidance, and wisdom. You thank her, knowing she is always there for you. Just a thought away.

After you bring yourself back, take some time to write about the insights you've had.

Courage is not the absence of fear, but rather the judgment that something else is more important than fear.

—Ambrose Redmoon, author

Loving Compassion

Often what we think of as compassion is really nothing more than judgment and pity in disguise. True compassion can only be felt with an open heart free of judgment and fear.

Imagine standing facing yourself. You see a cloud of sadness and pain surrounding your heart, so you breathe it in and replace it with love. As you breathe in the pain and sadness, you transform it into love. You continue to breathe in the sadness and pain until the cloud around your heart shimmers with the magic of love. And you feel free.

Now imagine your closest friend standing in front of you, and she, too, has a cloud around her heart. You breathe in her pain and replace it with love. You smile broadly at her as you fill her with love. She smiles and begins to fill you full of love as well.

Next, you stand in the presence of the creator of the universe, and that creative force begins to breathe you full of love. And you allow it to fill you totally and completely.

Next, imagine someone you dislike standing in front of you. He, too, has a cloud of sadness around his heart, and you have a cloud of judgment in your heart when you think of him. You begin to breathe him full of love, and with each breath, you let go of just a little more judgment until both of you are bathed in love.

In this chapter, you began to realize the importance of clear communication. You also got to see how your filter system distorts your experience of reality. You understand the power of choice and practice choosing love.

Chapter 12

Love Is

The book *A Course in Miracles* (see Appendix A) says that we only have two choices, love or fear, and fear is an illusion, and only the love is real. Love is not only a powerful emotion. Love causes us to expand energetically—we feel bigger and more expansive—while fear causes us to contract. Love is an incredibly powerful tool for healing emotionally, physically, and mentally. When we see life through the eyes of love, we see an entirely different world, and as a result, we make very different choices.

When you go through life knowing you have more than enough of everything, you can give freely of yourself and everything you have. When you are afraid you won't have enough, you feel the need to defend what you have and make sure no one takes it. Sharing freely isn't possible, and your choices are severely limited. Love makes the world go around, but it also makes it a wonderful place to live!

When fear haunts our thinking, the world lurking behind our choices is a very different place, devoid of true, expansive love. Fear colors our relationship with time, money, and relationships, including the one with our body and, in turn, our health.

Love and Fear

It is amazing how freeing love is and how drastically fear can distort your vision of life. Most of your habitual thinking and reactions to people, places, and things are based on fear. Next time you want to argue with someone you love or react to an event in your life, notice how fear is lurking, right there under the surface.

Judgment is always based on fear. Let me repeat that: All judgment is fear based. Love enables us to see the connections and explore the similarities. Fear causes us to focus on the differences. You don't need to use judgment to make decisions. You can learn to make your choices from a place of love instead.

Love invites you to embrace a life free of limitations. You can explore life and freely ask yourself, "What do I want?" knowing you can have it!

Eyes of Love

What we experience in life depends on our perspective and is only vaguely related to the event itself. If we start from a place of judgment, what we experience isn't even remotely the same as when we start from a place of love. If you don't like cats, for example, watching two kittens play will affect you very differently than a person who loves cats.

When you change your perspective, your experience changes. Hopefully, by now, you are beginning to realize how important it is to change your perspective.

This meditation will give you the opportunity to play with the idea of seeing life through the eyes of love.

You pick up a diamond-studded pair of glasses and hold them up to the light. They are beautiful, and the world looks different when you look through them.

At first, you aren't sure what the difference is, but you are curious, so you put them on. You take a deep breath and feel freer than you've ever felt before.

You look more closely at the room around you, and the colors are brighter, and everything looks sharper. You take the glasses off, and the colors seem dull.

You put the glasses on again and look in the mirror to see how they look on you. You are surprised that you can't see them at all. You decide to wear them.

When you start driving, you notice you are more thoughtful of other drivers. It feels good.

By the time you get to work, you feel a deep sense of connection to everyone. Things that might have bothered you before make you smile.

The world looks different. You simply feel more expansive, relaxed, and at ease.

By midday, you realize you are seeing the world through the eyes of love. Instead of feeling separate and alone, you feel connected to everyone.

Making your choices based on love is so easy. When you watch others responding in fear, you notice how their energy contracts.

You take a deep breath, notice how expansive your energy feels, and give thanks.

Whenever you want to see life through the eyes of love, you realize all you need do is ask yourself, "What would love do?"

Repeat this meditation often. Look in the mirror and imagine yourself putting on your rose-colored glasses.

When you find yourself upset, just take a deep breath and imagine love infusing your thoughts. Really bathe yourself in love.

Use your mind to change judgment and fear into the limitless energy of love.

When we feel love and kindness toward others, it not only makes others feel loved and cared for, but it helps us also to develop inner happiness and peace.

—Dalai Lama

Smile, Simply Smile

You may have heard that it takes fewer muscles to smile than it does to frown. When you smile, your body produces different peptides (chemicals), and you feel better. This meditation is a great way to start your day.

It is early in the morning, and you are slowly waking up. You smile as you realize you have the gift of another day.

You have a whole day ahead of you to fill with happiness and joy or trauma and drama. You decide to fill your day with joy.

You take a deep breath, and your smile deepens. From the tips of your toes to the top of your head, you smile with every cell of your being, and it feels great.

You get up and say good morning to yourself in the mirror. There is a twinkle in your eyes and a smile in your heart.

You smile broadly as you think about the day ahead of you, and you are filled with gratitude. As you move through the day, you pause occasionally and take time to let your spirit smile through you.

These meditations are mental exercises. The more you practice, the easier they become. The first time I did yoga, I was very stiff. The next day my body had lots of aches and pains.

But as I kept going, it got easier. These meditations do the same thing for your mind.

I wake up slowly each morning. If I let my mind wake up first, I can worry about life. I can change that thought and instead have a sense of wonder and expectancy for the day ahead.

Focusing on expansive, loving thoughts makes such a difference. The meditations you have the most resistance to are likely to be the ones that will make the most difference in your life. So, do them often.

How often each day do you stand in front of a mirror? Use that time to affirm how wonderful you. Look into your eyes and say, "I love you just the way you are! You are love, you are loved, and you are lovable. You are perfect just the way you are."

You get the idea; counter any negative thought or belief you might have. Mirror how you want to feel rather than how you may have thought to feel.

Floating

Here on the Big Island, we had warm ponds. They are saltwater ponds fed by underground spring water heated by the volcano. They were used by the Hawaiians as places of healing. A few years ago, the lava covered them up along with a lot of other magical places.

But this meditation will allow you to soak in them and experience their magic. It will help you let go of any tension, cares, or concerns.

You stand at the edge of the water. You can feel the warmth of the water radiating up from the pond. The moon has just risen, and it creates a ribbon of light on the surface of the water. The palm trees gently sway, and the stars twinkle overhead.

You slowly walk into the pond and are immediately embraced by the water. The saltwater is very buoyant, so you lie back and allow the water to support you.

You float effortlessly along, amazed at how relaxed you feel. You can feel the love that fills this place of healing, and you open your heart and mind to its healing power.

You float, embraced by the warmth of the water, and filled with the shimmering light of the moon. You had no idea life could be so good, and you could feel so full of love and peace.

Your mind, body, and spirit feel totally connected, whole, and complete. You allow the magic of the night to touch your heart and soul.

Love is the master key that opens the gates of happiness.

—Oliver Wendell Holmes, writer and physician

Love Can Move Mountains

When you look at the history of humans, the power of love and hate is very evident.

If you think about your own life, what effects have love, fear, and judgment had?

How much of your love has been unconditional, and how much of it has been fear-based?

Would you like to be able to love without the fear of being hurt?

Would you like to love in a more expansive manner?

What do you want to experience?

What do you want to create in relation to love?

The Ice Cube and the Hot Cup of Tea

Love can dissolve fear, or it can create more fear when it is fear-based love. It all depends upon what we tell ourselves. If you are willing to love, simply love, miracles happen.

Practice loving freely, with an open heart, and see what happens. You can use this meditation to easily and effortlessly change your perspective.

Imagine that you are a hot cup of tea that has just been freshly poured. Steam is floating off the cup, carrying the scent of the tea with it. The steam curls and twirls, drifting upward until it seems to disappear. You feel so warm and cozy.

Really see and experience yourself as a cup of tea. What would it be like to be a cup of tea?

Now imagine you are a medium-size ice cube. You are cold, and your edges are sharp. When you are removed from the freezer, a mist floats up off your surface, much like the steam from the hot cup of tea, but it's cold and icy.

Notice what it feels like to be a cold, ice-blue frozen chunk of water.

Listen as the ice cube is plunged into the hot cup of tea. The ice cube crackles and pops as it rapidly melts. The ice cube seems to have disappeared, but it merely changed forms. The tea is cooler, the ice cube warmer, and they are one.

They have changed each other. Feel yourself within the confines of the cup, gently being a cup of tea with no place to go and no place you need to be.

Trust

When I begin working with students, I tell them not to trust me. When I say that, the students often look shocked. It isn't about being cynical or believing "No one can be trusted." I explain that if they put their trust in me, in society, in another person, or their mind, they will always be disappointed.

But, if instead, they learn to listen to their spirit and place their trust in that innate, inner wisdom, they will never be disappointed. Trust is an internal journey. Trusting yourself is empowering and very freeing. No one has your answers except you.

Trust can be defined as placing confidence in someone or something. How much more empowering when you place that confidence in yourself instead of giving it away and hoping it works out!

This meditation gives you an opportunity to play with the idea of trust and gain a new understanding of it.

You have a beautiful coin in your hand. One side of the coin has the image of a beautiful eagle flying over a mountain range, majestic and free. On the other side is a single word, "trust," in big, bold, raised letters.

This is a very valuable coin. Each person has a coin like this, but often they are given away, lost, or not seen for a very long time.

You hold the coin close to your heart and feel the warmth of the love it contains. You allow the feeling of trust to fill your heart.

You take a deep breath and realize what a gift trust is. You know beyond a shadow of a doubt that you can trust your spirit's wisdom.

This is a coin for you and you alone. It is something for you to nurture and care for.

As you deepen that understanding, you realize you can trust yourself to make wonderful decisions. You know who to trust and that you can trust them without giving them the burden of caring for your coin.

You are free to carry your own coin, and so is everyone else. How freeing and expansive that feels.

Oddly enough, when I have a hard time making a choice, I use a coin—just a regular coin. I decide what each side stands for, and then I flip the coin. If it comes up heads and I want to flip it a few more times, I still have my answer. It works for me; give it a try for yourself. See how it feels to trust chance.

Love and Laughter

Love and laughter generally go hand in hand. When fear is present, anger, sadness, and disappointment aren't far behind. Learning how to love freely and without limits is a process that takes time, lots of practice, courage, and an open heart.Love really is safe. The only one who can take it away from us is ourselves.

Love Comes and Goes

Loving and being in love are often two different things. Sadly, at the end of a relationship, we often transmute what was once love into judgment, anger, and sometimes, even hate. If you are willing, the transition can be much gentler, easier, and less traumatic.

We can see our judgment for what is—fear in another disguise. We can let go of love and practice letting go of our fear-based judgments.

I find writing letters, ones that we never send, helps. Let out the judgment and pain; write it down with the intent of letting it go. When you feel done, write another letter while answering the question: How can I see this through the eyes of love?

One of my students felt particularly wronged, so she wrote a letter to her ex, tore it into pieces, threw it into the toilet, and then flushed it.

One common mistake is to think that one reality is THE reality. You must always be prepared to leave one reality for a greater one.

—Mother Meera, spiritual teacher

When you are at the end of one event, you are at the beginning of another journey. Allow your journeys to be ones of love. Every day, pick one meditation and just think about it throughout the day. Whenever you have a few moments, daydream about the meditation. This will help you let go of your old, limiting thinking and begin to enjoy life more fully while beginning to think more expansively.

Changing Address

My Hawaiian teacher calls dying "changing address." She is very connected to her ancestors and those who have passed over. Once I released my limiting beliefs about death, I no longer felt a deep sense of loss when someone died. I can often feel my mother's presence in a much more powerful way and absolutely know her love lives on.

If a friend goes on a trip, even though he might not be physically present, he is still in your heart and in your mind. When people die, they leave their bodies, but the essence of who and what they are lives on. They really are simply in the other room. If someone close to you dies and you are feeling sad about their passing, allow yourself to have your grief.

Once we start to have an emotion, it is too late not to have one. Allow your emotions to come and go. Make your emotions welcomed and honored guests in your life, but don't let them move in permanently. This is a beautiful meditation that will help you see death from a new perspective.

Take a deep breath and imagine yourself on the one side of a rainbow bridge. It connects this life with the next. The bridge is translucent, and as you stand there, you can see the other side very clearly.

When you travel over that rainbow bridge, you realize that you leave behind all your cares and concerns, regrets, and guilt. By the time you reach the other side, you are happy and free. You can see your life as an incredible gift, as an opportunity to remember who and what you really are.

You have no fear as you look at that bridge, just a deep sense of wonder, awe, and gratitude. You are grateful to be alive and to be able to see your friends on the other side.

You are relieved to know that this part of the journey is as magical as the rest. What a glorious way to end the wonderful experience that is called life.

Adrift in a Sea of Love

This meditation gives you the opportunity to see how your perspective affects your experience of life and how as your perspective changes, so does your ability to make choices.

You are adrift in the middle of the ocean. There are huge 20-foot swells, and you bob up and down with the waves.

You realize this can be an ocean filled with hungry sharks swimming around you, filling you with terror, or it can be an ocean of love that safely supports you. You take a long, slow, deep breath and decide it is an ocean of love.

As you bob up and down with the waves, you can't really see anything other than water. You see a small orange rubber raft and climb into it.

As you ride to the top of a wave, you can see just a little bit farther, and to your amazement, you see the mast of a sailboat. You climb into the sailboat, and the ocean still looks vast and empty.

Your magical journey on this sea of love continues to unfold, and a large ocean liner spots your little sailboat.

They pull up alongside you and bring you aboard. From the deck of the ocean liner, you can see the faint outline of the coast off in the distance. You would never have seen it from your sailboat, and the wind is blowing offshore.

On the deck of the ocean liner is a large helicopter. You step in, and as it rises into the air, you see a chain of islands and the mainland up ahead.

What a difference perspective makes. You can see dolphins and hundreds of boats and lots of people laughing and waving to you. This truly is a sea filled with magic and love.

In this chapter, we explored perspective, trust, and love. We also learned to see death as a change of address rather than an ending. We looked at love as an energy that can change your life profoundly.

Part 4

So, Now What?

Change occurs as soon as you are willing to let go of your old, limiting beliefs, agreements, attitudes, and assumptions. Once you become willing to see life differently, nothing changes—and yet, everything changes.

Would you like magic and miracles to become everyday occurrences? They can be if you use the meditations in this book on a regular basis.

The more often you immerse yourself in the concepts in these meditations, the more amazing your life will become. Read on, apply the concepts you're reading about, and enjoy the journey!

Chapter 13

Sweet Surrender

I never let go of anything without a fight. For years I resisted the idea of surrendering. I thought of surrendering as the ultimate failure.

As I deepened my understanding of mindfulness and meditation, I realized surrender was a necessary step. The more I played with the idea of surrender, I realized that all I was letting go of was my limited perspective, fear-provoking beliefs, as well as stress and struggle.

I watch people resist doing the very things that will set them free. To achieve real freedom in life, we each need to let go of our old beliefs, agreements, attitudes, and assumptions. Ironically, when we hold on to those beliefs, the result is our own misery. We often hold on to what's familiar rather than trying something new that might just set us free.

Surrender your old way of doing things so you can set yourself free.

Resistance Is Futile

The words used to define *surrender* in the dictionary are to give up, abandon, or relinquish. Those concepts didn't sound very positive, but surrendering is one of the most courageous and powerful things you can do. Every time we see life through our old, limiting filter system, we are arguing for our limitations.

In the context of personal growth, surrender is a very expansive and freeing concept. The ego-self, or the mind, is very tenacious, but when you surrender to the guidance of your true self, spirit, or inner essence, you can begin to experience your limitless nature.

Using the meditations in this book on a regular basis will change your life dramatically. Have you had any resistance to using the meditations? Any meditation that you just skimmed over and didn't do? Using the ones you have the most resistance to will be the most freeing. Surrender will set you free. It helps to realize that what you are surrendering to is your limitless nature. It isn't some unknown force wanting you to follow a set of rules; it is your spirit, the energy that gives you life.

So when you feel yourself resisting something, just let go, and do it anyway; try doing something new. To experience life in a limitless manner, you first must stop arguing for your limitations.

Really Letting Go

You can let go of something with your hand facing up. Theoretically, you've let go, but you are still holding on to it. Or you can turn your hand over and really let go.

The same is true of life: you can let go of a limiting belief by modifying it or really let it go. This meditation enables you to practice letting go.

Take a long, slow, deep breath and feel your chest as it expands. Exhale and slowly let go of that breath. Feel your breath as the air leaves your chest. Now inhale again and focus your attention on your chest as it fills with air.

When your lungs are full, hold your breath. Notice what it feels like to hold onto your breath. Hold your breath as long as you can, and then let go. Take another deep breath, exhale fully, and then hold your breath.

Notice what it feels like to resist allowing air back into your lungs. Avoid breathing for as long as possible.

Imagine holding a coin in the palm of your hand with your fist tightly closed around it. When you open your hand, the coin is still there. Now turn your hand over and feel as the coin effortlessly falls away.

You find yourself holding a beautiful helium balloon. It is a colorful butterfly. The sun glistens off its surface as it twirls effortlessly on the bright yellow cord. You watch the balloon as it bobs up and down.

You let go of the string, but it has a weight on the cord, so it hovers in front of you. You gently reach out and untie the weight, setting the balloon free.

Take a deep breath and notice what it felt like to hold your breath and let it go.

Notice what it felt like to hold on to the coin and let it go. What did it feel like to release the balloon and watch it fly away?

Imagine yourself letting go of your old limiting beliefs. Really let them go, with an open heart and an open mind, fully surrendering any of your old limitations. Imagine setting yourself free. Allow yourself to know at a very deep level what it feels like when you have let go and when you are only pretending to let go. Allow yourself to feel the freedom brought by true surrender.

Fluffing Your Aura

One of my students was having a difficult time finding a job after completing her medical residency. I suggested she do the following visualization.

Before going into an interview, she'd do the visualization in the bathroom. She'd been struggling for months, but before she knew it, she had several jobs to choose from. You can use this meditation to give yourself a boost of self-confidence whenever you need one.

Imagine yourself surrounded by a big ball of glowing light. You begin to look around, and you realize your energy, the essence of who and what you are, extends far beyond your physical body.

Your aura, that energy field around you, looks like a beautiful moving symphony of rainbow-colored lights.

Inside that bubble, you can see all your thoughts and feelings. Your energy field changes colors when you feel angry, happy, sad, limited.

You take a deep breath and imagine yourself making the bubble bigger and bigger until it fills the entire room. You see it full of all your favorite colors.

You play with the size of your aura, making it bigger and smaller. You change its color by merely thinking about it.

You breathe in and fill your energy field with self-confidence, joy, happiness, and a feeling of being connected to everyone and everything.

You fill your aura with a profound feeling of being safe no matter what. You enjoy playing with your energy field. You are grateful it is so easy and effortless. You know creating whatever you want is merely a thought away.

You have to count on living every single day in a way you believe will make you feel good about your life so that if it were over tomorrow, you'd be content with yourself.

—Jane Seymour, actress

In life, we aren't guaranteed tomorrow or the next moment. We only have this moment. Savor each moment. You can be worried and sad or happy and confident. The choice is yours, moment by moment. Savor each moment fully.

Pulling Energy from the Earth

For years, I hated hiking. Then one day, instead of going hiking, I went for a naturewalk and realized just how magical it could be.

That simple change, switching from hiking to going for a walk, changed everything. I've loved hiking ever since. Is there something you hate doing that you might like if you changed the way you thought about it?

As I connected with the earth and used the energy that abounds in nature, I found hiking invigorating. You can use this meditation to energize yourself when you are feeling tired, and you can also use it to connect more fully with nature.

You are walking on a dusty path on the side of a mountain. The wind is gritty and hot as it sweeps in off the desert. As the path climbs higher and higher, you move in and out of the shade. You pause and drink deeply from the cool water in your water bottle.

You look out at the vast expanse of the desert below you and feel a sense of connection. The wind talks to you, reminding you that you are part of the greater whole.

You find a beautiful outcropping and sit down to rest. You fall asleep and begin to dream.

Grandfather lizard begins to speak to you. He reminds you that when you take time to connect to the Earth Mother, she willingly gives you not only her wisdom but also her strength and the limitless energy contained within her domain.

He tells you to look at the palms of your hands. That is how you connect with the earth. You hold your hands out, and you can feel the energy of the desert filling you. When you move your hands up and down, you feel like a puppeteer. You feel like there are strands of energy attached to your hands, and it feels wonderful to play with it.

You awaken and see a small lizard scurrying away from you. At first, you are startled, but then you smile. You get up and begin hiking again.

This time the earth supports you as you move effortlessly up the mountain. As you play with the idea of pulling energy in through your hands, you realize you can do it anywhere, even in the middle of the city or in the heart of a building.

Making Life Easy

Life can be easy or hard. Life doesn't change for that to happen; all we need to do is change what we tell ourselves. You can think of life as a struggle in which you must learn lessons and pass tests, or you can view life as an opportunity to connect with your divine nature. Each moment you can choose to connect with your limitless nature or your small, limited self. Whenever you are struggling, it's a safe bet you've connected with your limited self.

When magic and miracles aren't everyday occurrences, you aren't connected to your divine self, and it is time to make another choice. When judgment is present, so is fear. Your spirit knows no fear, while your limited, small self knows no peace. Your only two choices are love and fear. When you find yourself judging, take a few moments to focus on loving yourself and accept your choices unless you'd rather remain miserable.

Slowing Your Thoughts

Chances are, your thoughts are racing when you are immersed in your filter system or when your small, limited fear-based self has taken over. Thoughts seem to come out of nowhere, and before you know it, you are focused on them.

This is a great meditation to use whenever you want to quiet your mind and is very useful when you need help falling asleep.

Take a long, slow, deep breath. Focus your attention on your thoughts. What were you thinking?

Observe your thoughts as they come into your mind. Are the thoughts loving and expansive or fearful and annoying?

Notice if any catch your attention or if you forget you are just observing your thoughts.

Take a deep breath and just keep bringing yourself back to your thoughts.

Speed your thoughts up. Make them go very, very fast. Mentally talk very fast to yourself until the words are just a constant humming.

Now take a deep breath and begin to slow your thoughts. Talk very slowly.

Pronounce each letter of each word and just slow your thoughts down. Think a word, then pause, and then think another word. Think slowly and methodically. Pause your thoughts for a moment and then begin thinking again slowly.

Now think rapidly again. Speed up your thoughts until they are again just a mental blur. Then gently slow them down again until you are thinking one letter and one word at a time. Speak internally in a very calm, slow, patient, and loving voice.

Practice speeding up your thoughts and slowing them down until you can easily do it whenever you want, at will.

> You have powers you never dreamed of. You can
> do things you never thought you could do. There
> are no limitations in what you can do except the
> limitations of your own mind.
>
> —Darwin Kingsley, author

Embracing Change

Change can be a fearful or a fun-filled adventure. It all depends on what we tell ourselves. When I graduated from college, I decided I didn't like change and tried to avoid it at any cost. During my years at college, my parents separated and got back together numerous times. My mom tried to kill herself and never regained the use of one of her hands. Change became a thing to avoid. I made myself miserable until I realized change was inevitable, and I could either enjoy it or hate it.

Once I embraced it and stopped fearing and judging it, I could make more loving choices. Change became an invitation to expand and create something more expansive and loving.

What looks like death to the caterpillar is birth to the butterfly. Once again, your perspective dictates your experience. This meditation helps you embrace change and see it from a different perspective.

Allow change to become a joyous and expansive experience, something to look forward to. Take a few moments to relax, and imagine yourself standing on a hill looking down at a beautiful, ancient-looking town.

You walk into an old village. You are tired and thirsty, and in the center of the town square, there is a beautiful fountain.

There is an old woman, her face deep with lines and filled with kindness, standing next to the fountain. When she looks into your eyes, you feel like you have known her all your life.

She reaches out and hugs you. A tear of joy trickles down her face, and with the sweetest voice you have ever heard, she says, "Welcome. I am so glad you finally made it. We've been waiting for you; welcome home." She hands you an ornate gourd filled with cold, clear water, and you drink deeply. You have never tasted water so fresh and felt so alive. You say "thank you" and ask for some more.

A young child offers to take your backpack. As you remove it, you realize it was very heavy, and the straps had been cutting into your shoulders. It feels good to let go of the burden.

The old woman looks at you and says, "Child, for many years, you have been carrying burdens, sadness, cares, and concerns, and it is time to let go. This is a place you can come to let go of anything that no longer serves you. Life is meant to be a joyous experience. When you release your limiting thoughts, when you surrender to the flow of life, magic happens. This is a place of great magic. Welcome."

She leads you over to a colorful hammock and invites you to lie down. You fall asleep almost immediately, and when you awaken, it is dark, and the sky is filled with millions of stars. The air is fresh and cool.

You are hungry, and there is a table overflowing with all your favorite dishes. You feel blessed.

You see people gathering in the square, and you go over to join them. There is a big fire burning, and the old woman invites you to throw all your cares and concerns into the fire.

She tells you to throw away your fear of change and to know the only thing that is real is the magic. When you look into her eyes, you know it is true, and you feel freer than you have ever felt before. Change, indeed, can be as easy as letting go.

You look into the eyes of the people around you, and you see only love, joy, and happiness. You hear lots of laughter.

You join others as they do a happy dance, feeling the freedom that now lies within your heart and your mind. You find the old woman; she hugs you, and you are so grateful to have her in your life.

You intuitively know you can come back here any time, and she will be waiting. She will help you let go of whatever no longer serves you.

Every man is his own ancestor, every man is his
own heir. He devises his own future and inherits
his own past.

—Frederic Henry Hedge, author and Harvard professor

Cutting the Ties That Bind

Everything in this world is energy. You, me, a building, the earth, and
even this book you are reading are all made up of atoms. At a core level,
everything is made up of stardust.

Some spiritual traditions believe that there are fibers of light connecting
us to everyone we have ever met and every place we have ever been. You
can use this simple meditation to free yourself from the past or anything
that no longer serves you.

*You are standing in a beautiful room filled with a brilliant white light.
You stand in the very center of the room, feeling incredibly free, at
peace, and at ease. In your hand is a magical pair of scissors.*

*As you look around your body, you see hundreds of fine filaments of
light that look almost like a spider web connecting you to your past.*

*You see how they constrict your movement, so one by one, you
slowly begin to cut them away.*

*You feel freer and freer, more and more alive, as you cut each of
the strands of light.*

*You begin to laugh and feel joy welling up within you. You wonder
why you never thought to do this before, and you give thanks for the
opportunity to do it now.*

It is a very simple visualization. As you move through your day and feel
upset, you can mentally cut the cords to that upset. A wonderful practice
is to review the day before you go to sleep, releasing anything that caused
disharmony. You could imagine yourself erasing it or just cutting the
cord. Forgive, forget, and fill that spot with love.

Being Happy

You are only as happy as you make up your mind to be. I have a message on my answer machine that says I hope you have a nice day unless you already have plans otherwise.

Before I did some brainwashing, I was angry when anyone suggested I could be happy if I wanted to be. I was too attached to my stories of misery and suffering to be happy.

Psychologists and scientists rarely study the causes of happiness. Often, people habitually focus on being unhappy and then create more unhappiness. You can choose to move away from pain and toward pleasure. If you choose to move away from pain, you will keep creating pain to move away from.

Make sure you focus on what you do enjoy. Create a list of things that really make you happy, and do at least one of those things every day.

Things happen in life. Parents die, relationships come and go, people get sick, and cars break down. The question is, "What are we going to tell ourselves about those events?"

Emotions can be great fun, and we can express a different emotion whenever we want. Enjoy your sadness, savor your anger, and embrace your joy. Then decide how you want to feel and create that emotion as well.

Life is an incredibly sensual experience, and there is no reason to deny any of it or get stuck, either. Happiness is always just a thought away, as is misery or anger or—well, you get the idea.

Some days, you feel like eating chocolate, and some days, you want broccoli. There is no need to make yourself eat broccoli if you really want chocolate!

Becoming a Tree

The more you use your imagination, the easier it will be for you to create what you want, when you want it. I used to suffer from chronic depression until I realized I could exchange misery for joy.

(As always consult with your physician before making any changes. Depression can be serious or life threatening.)

This meditation will help you exercise your imagination while enabling you to see life from a different perspective.

Imagine yourself as a tall and graceful tree. Your branches spread out, creating a wonderful, shaded area at your feet.

You can feel your roots going deep into the earth, bringing up nutrients and grounding you. Your roots go deeper and deeper into the earth, giving you a profound sense of connection.

You feel so alive. Your branches reach up toward the sun, gently moving with the wind.

Birds live in your branches. You act as a home for many creatures, large and small. You flow with the seasons. As summer turns into fall, your leaves turn beautiful colors and then fall off.

Your branches rustle magically with the wind all winter long. When the warmth of the sun returns in the spring, your branches swell with blossoms that rapidly turn into supple leaves.

Take a deep breath and feel as the sap flows from your roots into your leaves. You feel the life flowing through your entire being.

You look around at the world and see time gently moving forward. You feel the grace with which life moves through you. Relax back into the freedom of being a tree.

Aging

We live in a society that worships youth and judges and fears aging. Aging is a natural part of life and can be a wonderful experience. Many people would argue that aging beats the alternative of dying.

When I turned 50, I realized I had no positive mental images of myself at 60 or 70. I could easily imagine myself being a feisty old lady but had no clear images of how I would get there.

This meditation is an invitation for you to embrace aging. Allow it to be fun and create some positive mental images of yourself as you age.

Imagine yourself standing in front of a magic mirror. When you look at the mirror, you can easily move forward and back in time. With a mere thought, you can see yourself at any age.

First, you see yourself shortly after your birth. You are surrounded by beautiful beings of light that are constantly beaming you their love. As time passes, you feel their love and their guidance.

Your conscious choice to connect with them makes your life much easier and more joyous. Even the most painful times are filled with ease and have an undercurrent of excitement, curiosity, and joy.

Time passes, and you see your body changing. You celebrate the wisdom these changes bring. You look lovingly at yourself in the mirror.

You notice a lovely light that comes from within you, shining out of your eyes and into your life. You notice your face changing and feel joy at the gentle aging process. You see the wrinkles on your face as symbols of your journey rather than something to resent, and you give thanks for the passage of time.

You see yourself moving into your sixties. Your body is slowing down a bit, but it is still a wonderful vehicle for your spirit. You notice your body aging with grace and realize the more you love the process, the easier it is.

You send your body lots of love. You love every single wrinkle and gray hair.

The more you love the process, the more flexible your body becomes.

As you look at this magical mirror, you see the connections between love, acceptance, and judgment. You see the results graphically in your body, so you choose love and acceptance.

What a gift life is. What an incredible gift it is to have a body and to celebrate your body's ability to change with age. Aging is one of life's greatest gifts if you embrace the process.

How would your life have been different if you had done this meditation as a child? You can change the past as easily as you can the present. Time is fluid. Permit yourself to change what was so you can change what is.

In this chapter, we explored the power of surrender and of letting go of what was. We explored perspective, embraced change, and began to realize how changing our perspective to one of love can transform life.

Chapter 14

Magic Happens

"Magic happens" isn't just some New Age slogan. Miracles aren't reserved for a chosen few. When you learn to take full responsibility for your life, connect at a profound level to the essence of who and what you really are, magic and miracles become part of your everyday life. As your perspective changes, so do your choices, and then the magic begins.

When I began my journey, I waited for the magic. I saw the lives of people around me change, and mine didn't. I struggled so hard, and in hindsight, I realize all my suffering was unnecessary. I never surrendered control and fully took responsibility for my choices. Once I did, everything changed, and nothing changed.

My life became a series of incredibly magical, miraculous events. And your life can be, too. Just use these meditations, let go of your old limiting beliefs, and surrender to the innate wisdom of your spirit. It takes discipline and dedication to change your thinking. I assure you, that effort is well worth the results you will get.

Your Limitless Nature

You really are limitless. Magic and miracles can be everyday occurrences. The only thing that limits you is your filter system, beliefs, agreements, attitudes, and assumptions. You can create whatever you want when you want. Everything is in your life by invitation, and anything not in your life isn't there because, at some level, you haven't invited it yet. You are 100 percent responsible for everything in your life, and you are not at fault.

What is magic? What constitutes a miracle? Both really are in the eyes of the beholder. So often, when we think of magic, we think of books like the *Harry Potter* series instead of something as mundane as taking the time to see a rainbow when others are walking by, oblivious to its beauty.

After I completed my apprenticeship with Don Miguel Ruiz and Mother Sarita, I would periodically go back to San Diego to spend some time with them. During one of my visits, Don Miguel told me I had a lot of knowledge, and now my task was to turn it into wisdom. When I asked him what that meant, he smiled, changed the subject, and began talking about something totally unrelated. It took me a while to understand the difference. It is subtle, and the change in my life was tremendous. Humans love accumulating knowledge but seldom take the time to embrace wisdom.

If you've worn glasses for your entire life that totally distort reality, the only reality you know and can see is distorted. The same is true of your filter system. When I speak before a large group and talk about responsibility, people ask questions that make it very clear they have confused fault and responsibility, and they believe there is such a thing as good and bad.

Everything in life is an opportunity for you to strengthen your connection with your filter system or your spirit. When you see things as bad, you align your thoughts with your filter system. When you remember that everything is perfect, that everything is pono, you are surrendering to the wisdom of your spirit.

Ways of Being

We can be open to an experience or closed. We can see the world through eyes willing to see the limitless possibilities or only willing to focus on the limitations.

If you walk right up to a wall and put your nose against it, all you can see is the wall. Your filter system is like that; it stops you from seeing anything beyond its limited version of reality.

This meditation enables you to open to a variety of ways of being.

You find yourself walking around a huge old house. It has lots and lots of rooms, and each one is unique.

You walk into an old-fashioned living room. The lace curtains hung in the windows billow gracefully as the wind blows in.

As you walk, you feel loved and at peace. When you sit on the couch, you feel very relaxed, and a deep sense of knowing fills you. You can feel the presence of an ancient wisdom, and you know it is yours for the asking.

You sit back, and the couch envelops you. The sunlight streams across the floor, and you feel at home and very welcomed. As you think about your life, you see the perfection and the limitless possibilities unfolding before you.

You take a deep breath and walk into the next room. It looks very cold and sterile. When you walk in, you feel ill at ease and restless. When you think about your life, you are filled with fear, and every choice seems like the wrong one. You don't stay very long.

The next room is painted a light green and filled with beautiful plants. The air is moist, fresh, and clean, and the sunshine filters through skylights in the ceiling.

You take a deep breath and feel a deep sense of connection to the wonder life holds. You could spend many hours here, but you are curious about the rest of the house, so you move on.

Each room is different, and each room evokes a deep feeling and way of being within you. As you enter each room, your perspective changes completely. You are amazed there are so many ways to view your life. As your perspective changes, you can see so many different, more expansive choices.

The idea of right and wrong begins to slip away. You begin to realize there are an infinite number of opportunities to make very different choices. Life simply gives you chances to make choices, to see the results, and then if you want different outcomes, to make different choices.

You walk into a room filled with a brilliant white light, and you are filled with gratitude. You realize your life can be filled with magic and miracles, trauma and drama, or a little bit of both.

You are the creator, and you get to make the choices, either consciously or unconsciously. You decide to choose love more often.

In order to make an apple pie from scratch, you must first create the universe.

—Carl Sagan, astronomer and writer

Cosmic Cappuccino

This meditation gives you a different vision of life and all the events in it. When I face a challenge, meditation helps me maintain my sense of humor and see possibilities I might not otherwise have seen.

You haven't been born yet. You are at the Cosmic Cappuccino House having a latte with all your friends. You are sitting around, talking about the opportunity to have a body and experience life. You decide you want to learn more about love, surrender, and your limitless nature. You know the moment you are born, you will forget all you know, this discussion, and the issues you want to play with, but that's okay.

You all sit around laughing, excited about the limitless possibilities. Each of you agrees to play different roles in one another's lives. The spirits closest to you agree to play the villains in your life. Only those who love you the most are willing to play the really difficult and challenging roles. Spirits that are acquaintances agree to play the easy roles that are less dramatic and less challenging.

You agree to meet one another at different points in each other's lives. Sometimes, you might agree just to bump into one another briefly, while others agree to play more long-term roles. Once the roles each of you will play are decided, you sit around and talk for an eternity, excited about the new adventures you are all about to embark upon.

Even though each of you knows you will forget as soon as you are born, you are thrilled with the idea of playing with issues and incarnating into a limited physical universe. Each of you will have an infinite number of opportunities to play with limitations and move beyond them or get stuck in them. Either way, it will be a wonderful adventure.

As you leave the coffeehouse, you wish each other good luck. You say goodbye, knowing that you will meet again soon. You might not remember you are meeting by divine appointment, but that doesn't matter. Everyone shows up at just the perfect moment.

You are off to have an incredible adventure in the universe's most wonderful amusement park, and you have everything you need to enjoy the process and have fun.

You Get What You See

Unless you believe it, you won't see it. If you expect to get ripped off, chances are you will. If you assume life is hard, you will have ample opportunities to struggle. We often think visually. Our minds are very busy having thoughts, imagining what might happen, or thinking about the past.

For a day, notice how often you are thinking about something other than what you are doing. Notice how often you are fully present, savoring the moment.

Whatever you focus your attention on, you get more of. You can drive down the street noticing all the wonderful things along your route, or you can focus on the litter. You can watch the news and think "how awful," or notice all the places needing love. The more you judge what is, the more you limit your choices and experience your limited self. The more you look for the magic and wonder of life, the more you will experience your limitless nature. You get more of what you choose to see.

When you find yourself waiting in line or stuck in traffic, mentally review one of the meditations. Use the time to submerge yourself in love. Ask yourself lots of questions. How can I see this through the eyes of love? Seeing through the eyes of love is my favorite. Use your mind to observe and create wonderful scenarios. Imagine the person next to you winning the lottery and using the money wisely.

Conscious Creation

You got where you are in life by thinking your habitual thoughts, mentally envisioning the same thing repeatedly, and making choices based on the same beliefs. You are constantly creating your experience of reality and inviting people, places, and things into your life.

You are the creator in your life: unless you are consciously choosing your creation, you are creating based on your filter system. The gift is as you expand your awareness of what's possible, the quality of your habitual thoughts will improve as well.

Just as the title of this section implies, this meditation shows you how to consciously create what you want. Take a few minutes to think of something you would like to create, then use this meditation on a regular basis until you create it.

Get a clear image of what you want to create. Think about what it would feel to have it. Think about how your life would change and how nice it would be to know you could create whatever you want, whenever you want it.

Take a few moments to really notice what that would feel like. How would your body feel if you absolutely had everything you wanted? Would your chest be full and open? How would your stomach feel? Imagine how your body would feel.

Take a moment and focus on the feeling of having rather than wanting to have. Get a clear mental image of having whatever it is you want to create.

If it is an object, imagine yourself holding it. If you want a new car, imagine yourself behind the wheel, driving, smiling, and at ease in your new car.

If you want a relationship, imagine feeling loved, going out together and having fun, laughing, loving, and enjoying being together.

If you want a lover, be the perfect lover. Take yourself out on a date, buy yourself flowers, leave sweet notes. Give thanks for all the love. Gratitude is the sweet, magic elixir of life.

Get a clear image of what you want to create, make sure you are in the image with it, feel it, know it, have it, and give thanks for it being in your life.

Daydream about having what you want as often as possible, knowing you already have it. Listen to your inner guidance and take concrete, actionable steps regularly.

Energy Balls

This is a fun way to play with creating and letting go without having to conjure up images. It is a guided meditation combined with some simple hand movements. Have fun!

Imagine holding your hands over your head and gathering up a big ball of energy. Keep gathering up energy like you're making a huge, cosmic snowball.

First, put anything you want to let go of into it. Put in all your limiting thoughts and feelings, any sense of struggle, and everything you would like to release.

When the ball is as full as it can possibly be, throw it up into the very heart of the universe. See it transform into a beautiful ball of glowing white light.

Next, hold your hands out in front of you and create another cosmic snowball. This time, fill it with love, joy, ease, and all your wishes, dreams, and desires. Pack them all into the ball until it is as full as it can possibly get.

Now gently place it in front of your chest and slowly push it into your heart until both your hands are touching your chest. Just gently hold your heart until you feel you are done.

This is a fun and easy visualization that can really make a difference.

Is the Cup Half Empty or Half Full?

Perspective is everything. In this meditation, you get to practice changing your perspective and observe what happens when you do.

You hold a magnificent glass in your hands. It shimmers with rainbows of light, and the liquid it contains glistens. You notice the liquid only fills part of the glass. You take a deep breath and have the thought that the glass is half empty.

As soon as you have that thought, the liquid begins to drain out of the glass. The rainbows left behind by the liquid enthrall you, and as the glass continues to slowly drain, you have the thought that perhaps the glass really was half full.

At that instant, the glass begins to fill again until the liquid is almost spilling over the top of the glass. You are amazed by the sudden transformation.

As you decide to play with your thoughts, you think of the glass as half empty, and the liquid once again drains out.

You think of it as half full, and sure enough, it begins to fill again. As you play with your thoughts, you notice that the glass fills and empties more rapidly when you add emotions to the mix.

You decide to feel incredibly grateful that the glass is half full; the liquid races to the top, and the rainbows intensify, filling the entire room.

For years, I worried about money and feared bankruptcy and losing everything. Eventually, I created the experience, but luckily, a bookstore had just opened in town that had lots of self-help and spiritual books.

I read and read and began to change my filter system.

One day, I went to court. The room was full. The judge came in and told us all to stand. He said a few things, and then he said, "You are all bankrupt."

It was a very emotional and pivotal moment in my life. Today, I live on the Big Island of Hawaii, own a beautiful home, write books, travel, have a wonderful family, and help others create the lives of their dreams.

Had I not stood in that courtroom and been declared bankrupt, none of that would have ever happened.

What Do You Want More of?

If you want peace of mind, avoiding the news may help temporarily, but being able to watch the news and remain centered and loving will help more in the long run. We can be so logical about some things and completely stubborn about other things.

Think about what you want more of and then ask yourself, "What sort of thoughts and actions would create that in my life? If I knew I already had what I wanted, what choices would I make?"

If you want abundance in your life, neither overspending nor telling yourself "I can't afford it," will create abundance. Living within your means and saying, "I choose not to buy that right now," while knowing you have more than enough, will.

Get clear about what you want more of and think thoughts that are consistent with having it. Having those thoughts as often as possible infused with a sense of knowing will make a big difference in your life.

Attitude of Gratitude

I had a hard time with the idea of gratitude when I first began my spiritual journey. I started on my journey because I was miserable, so I thought I had nothing to be grateful for.

Once I changed that belief, my life changed tremendously. For many years part of my practice was to write a list of everything I was grateful for each night before I went to bed. This meditation will help you get in touch with the power of gratitude. This is a wonderful meditation to do, especially when you don't think you have anything to be grateful for!

Take a long, slow, deep breath. As you breathe in, feel your heart expanding, filling with love, peace, and ease. As you breathe out, let go of anything unlike love, peace, and ease. Imagine yourself surrounded by a beautiful cloud of pink and green shimmering light.

The air glistens and dances magically. You are surrounded by millions of brilliant diamonds of glimmering light.

As you breathe in, your entire body is filled with the vibrant light. Your body relaxes, and at the same time, it feels totally and vibrantly alive.

You breathe in a profound sense of gratitude. You begin to look at your life through the eyes of gratitude, and everything is surrounded by lovely pinkish-green lights.

You breathe in gratitude and release anything unlike gratitude. You feel so peaceful and full of joy.

Mentally you make a list of everything you are grateful for. You feel the sense of gratitude building and growing until it flows over everything in your life, even the things you have judged in the past.

You find yourself being grateful for it all, everything, absolutely everything. When you feel judgment rising to the surface, you surround it with the pinkish-green light, and you immediately have gratitude for even that judgment.

You take a deep breath and give thanks.

Most folks are about as happy as they make up their minds to be.

—Abraham Lincoln

Focusing Your Attention

Whatever you focus your attention on, you get more of. This meditation is a wonderful exercise designed to help you consciously focus your attention.

You are standing in a pitch-black room. There is no light, none, and everything is dark. You have no idea where you are or if there is anything or anyone in the room with you.

You notice there is something in your hand, and you realize it is a large flashlight. You turn it on and begin to explore the room.

It is filled with wonderful treasures and hundreds of boxes. You explore them all with curiosity, excited by all the wonderful things you find.

Then you notice a window and shine your flashlight at it. You can really see outside, but you see an instrument panel nearby, neatly installed on the wall.

You turn on a beam of light and find you can easily direct it by manipulating one of the knobs. You can make the light brighter and broader or refine it until it is a powerful laser beam. You can adjust the light to see the details or take in large areas all at once.

As you play with the light, you begin to think about your life. You realize you can focus your attention broadly, you can look at the details, or you can remain in the dark.

You can focus on what you do want, or on not having what you want, or you can even focus on what you don't want. You realize that whatever you focus your attention on, that is what you get more of.

You enjoy playing with focusing your attention just as you did the light. The more you practice, the easier it becomes.

In this chapter, we explored how you can embrace magic and, in the process, vastly improve the quality of your life. Creation follows awareness and where you focus your attention. You realize how important love, acceptance, and gratitude are and invite them into your life more often.

Chapter 15

It's a Journey, Not a Destination

If you are busy worrying about where you are going, you don't get to enjoy where you are. The only regret I have about my life is I often failed to allow myself to enjoy every step of the journey. When I was first exploring meditation and spirituality, I wanted to be more advanced and never allowed myself to enjoy being at the beginning.

Wherever you are in your process, celebrate it. This is the only moment you can experience this moment. If you are struggling with using the meditations, celebrate the struggle. Wherever you are, you are there, so you may as well enjoy being there.

Actually Doing It

Life really is all about the journey and learning how to be fully present in the moment. The destination doesn't really matter. Over the years, hundreds of people have shared with me that they have read lots of books and taken numerous workshops, yet their lives are pretty much the same. When I ask them if they did the exercises, the answer is usually no.

Actually, using these meditations will make a difference in your life; thinking about using them won't. Set yourself up for success. Allow the process to be as easy as possible.

Procrastination used to be one of my biggest challenges. At one point, I realized that it takes more time to think about doing something than it takes to actually do it. So, just do it instead of thinking about doing it.

If you feel bad about yourself for not using the meditations, start telling yourself the truth. You are choosing to make yourself feel bad about yourself. Ask yourself if that is what you want to continue to create.

A journey is defined as the act of going from one place to another. Life can only be lived moment by moment. Your spiritual explorations are a process of expanding your awareness. This is a journey in which you find yourself and realize just how wonderful you are and always have been.

So, take the time to do the meditations, make your journey into wholeness or holiness an enjoyable one that is full of love, laughter, joy, and ease.

Expanding and Contracting

This is a very simple visualization. You can use it to change how you feel, as well as to change the nature of your relationship with the people, places, and things in your life.

If you are going for a job interview, make your energy field really big. When you sit down to pay your bills, see the bills being small, the money in your checking account being abundant, and your relationship to money supportive and easy.

Take a deep breath and feel your chest as it expands and contracts. Really focus on feeling your breath as your chest rises and falls.

Focus your attention on your back and notice how the back of your chest expands, too. Feel all the muscles in your chest as they move and how your chest effortlessly expands and contracts as the air moves in and out of your lungs.

Now imagine yourself expanding and contracting with your breath. See yourself getting bigger and smaller. With each breath, allow yourself to get a little bit bigger and smaller. Imagine yourself getting so big you fill the entire room, then your house, and then your entire state. With each breath, allow yourself to get bigger until you expand to encompass the entire planet.

Then allow yourself to get so small you could fit on the head of a pin. Just allow yourself to effortlessly get bigger and smaller.

Keep shifting your focus between getting large and small. Notice the subtle differences between getting large and small in your body and your breath.

Happiness is not in our circumstances but in ourselves. It is not something we see, like a rainbow, or feel, like the heat of a fire. Happiness is something we are.

—John Sheerin, actor

Listening to Your Heart

You can listen to the limitations of your filter system or to the innate wisdom of your heart. You will find that the more you listen to the guidance of your spirit, the more serendipity you will experience in your life. This meditation helps you open up those lines of communication.

Close your eyes and focus your attention on the center of your chest. Imagine yourself breathing in through your chest and out through the top of your head. Really focus your attention on your chest. Notice how it feels after you breathe in through your heart for a few minutes.

Imagine yourself settling back into your heart center. You take a deep breath and relax into your heart. It feels very comfortable, cozy, spacious, and familiar. You take a few more deep breaths and allow yourself to get really comfortable and relaxed.

You sit quietly in the center of your heart, just listening. Off in the distance, you hear a gentle whisper. It is a very loving voice that begins to speak to you. It reminds you of your perfection; it talks to you of love and acceptance and of joy and ease.

As you listen, you feel incredibly nurtured, safe, and loved. You feel the wisdom and the knowledge contained in that voice, and you give thanks for its presence in your life.

You breathe deeply, while you sink into the connection, allowing it to enfold you, embrace you, and surround you. You give thanks for the connection and know you can come here to access that wisdom whenever you want.

The more you practice listening to this loving wisdom, the easier it will be to let go of your filter system. When I began my journey, my filter system felt safe and comforting. Now it sounds like a raucous crow, annoying, limiting, and fear-based.

Learn from the mistakes of others. You can't live long enough to make them all yourself.

—Eleanor Roosevelt, writer,
delegate to the United Nations, and former first lady

Having It All

No matter what you want, you can have it if you make choices that are consistent with its creation. If you want peace of mind, you can easily have it if you choose to think peaceful thoughts. If you want to go to Los Angeles, you need to know where you are, how to get there, and then follow the directions. The same is true of anything in life.

If you want to feel loved, realize you might not love yourself unconditionally right now. Create statements that are accepting of yourself exactly how you are right now, and then consistently repeat those phrases, especially when you feel critical or unloving.

Here are four steps to creating what you want:

1. Be absolutely clear about what you do want.
2. Know where you are right now.
3. Clearly define all the steps necessary to get from here to there.
4. Moment by moment, take the appropriate actions.

Basically, your first step is to define your "it" in Having It All then create an inner dialog that will help you get there.

What Do You Really Want?

Knowing what you do want instead of what you don't want sometimes takes practice. For a few days, notice how often you say "I don't want this," or "I can't do that," or "I should do this." Those are all ways you sabotage yourself, and they won't help you get any closer to what you do want.

Part of knowing what you really want is looking at the goal behind the goal. Sometimes, people want more money because they think it will give them more leisure time. So, the goal behind the goal would be leisure time. This meditation facilitates you in finding the goal behind the goal.

Working long hours to make more money won't give you more free time. Focusing on creating more leisure time might allow you the time to see ways to make more money. So, find the real goal and focus on creating that!

Start by thinking about something you want. Take a deep breath and visualize it in great detail. Imagine the image of it in front of you and mentally turn it over and over. Look at it from all angles. Turn it upside down and look at it that way.

Think about it symbolically.

- What does it represent to you? Is it freedom, power, safety, or ease?
- What will having it do for you or to you?
- Think of just the word. Does that word best describe what you really want?
- Say the word silently over and over to yourself. How does it feel?
- Is the word expansive?
- How do you feel when you say it?
- What emotions do you feel when you think about really having it?
- Take a deep breath and ask it if it has a message for you.
- What would your desired outcome like to say to you?
- What would you like to say to it?

Let yourself know in the core of your being what you really want to have, and then give yourself permission to have it.

Letting It Be Easy

I constantly hear people talk about how hard life is. You can make life hard or easy. You can enjoy your process or struggle. The choice is entirely up to you. This meditation helps you practice allowing it to be easy.

When I was a senior in high school, our house burned down the day after Christmas and we lost everything. My family splintered and I was devastated. Fast forward: After I embraced many of the concepts I share in this book, I can experience the gift in that moment. Now I realize I didn't have to suffer at all.

Think about the word "easy." What does it feel like? Easily and effortlessly think about easy. Breathe in the feeling of easy, and breathe out easy. Mentally shake your body and release any tension, cares, or concerns.

Relax your shoulders and your neck. Allow your entire body to be filled with the feeling of easy. Just let go and surrender to the feeling of easy.

What does easy taste like? What would it sound like to hear yourself saying everything is easy? How would your friends feel if they knew everything came easily for you?

Imagine the feeling of everything being easy, filling you from head to toe. Imagine the feeling of it being easy pouring into the top of your head. It fills your legs, flows up into your stomach, and into your chest. It slowly flows into both of your arms. After it fills your head, it flows down over the outside of your body until you are surrounded by the feeling of it being easy. You are swimming in a sea of ease.

It is wrong to think that misfortunes come from the east or from the west; they originate within one's own mind. Therefore, it is foolish to guard against misfortune from the external world and leave the inner mind uncontrolled.

—Buddha

Say Yes

Sometimes, we struggle to say yes to the good things in life. Limiting ourselves and saying yes to struggle is simply more familiar.

Joyously saying yes to our ability to savor all of life takes practice. So, decide whether you want to practice saying yes or no. Neither answer is right or wrong; it all depends on what you want to experience in your life.

When I must decide—and I'm not sure what I want to do— I flip a coin. If it comes up heads and I want to go two out of three, I still have my answer.

Explore what saying yes to life would mean to you and what saying no means. Notice what your habitual choice is and choose something different for a change.

Surrendering to What You Want

When you walk across quicksand, the last thing you want to do is struggle unless you want to drown in the mud.

Fighting your mind or your filter system is pointless if you really want to be happy. Focusing on happiness works far better.

In this meditation, you get to play with the idea of surrendering to what you want instead of fighting with what you don't want.

You are standing on a very high platform. Far below you is a large, fully inflated pillow strategically placed to break your fall.

You are nervous as you stand at the edge of the platform, looking down. You are terrified at the thought of jumping, but you know it is the only way down and that you will feel so free after you jump.

You put your toes at the very edge of the platform and look down. Looking down takes your breath away. Your friends look like little ants waving up at you.

Their voices drift toward you, and you hear lots of words of encouragement and can feel their excitement for you.

You are very aware of the fact that you don't want to jump but that you do want to get down. They seem to be the antithesis of each other, and you realize you can focus on your fear and what you don't want, or on your freedom and what you do want.

You take a deep breath and imagine what it would feel like to surrender and just fall off the platform. You look around and become aware of the presence of your spirit there with you on the platform.

Your spirit lovingly reaches out and comforts you. It enfolds you and you feel incredibly safe and secure. You realize you could fly if you wanted to.

You step to the edge of the platform, turn around, put your arms out, and fall effortlessly backward off into space. As you fall, you feel exhilarated. You are absolutely free. You are flying.

The fall seems to last forever, but then you feel the pillow as it embraces you and slowly deflates to cushion your fall. You are so relieved. Your friends race over to congratulate you. You are so proud of yourself. You created exactly what you wanted and so much more. You smile and are grateful you didn't spend the rest of your life looking down at life. You are grateful you surrendered and allowed yourself to fly.

Freedom is always just a thought away.

Only in the darkness can you see the stars.

—Martin Luther King Jr.

On Temporary Loan

Everything in life is only on temporary loan. Buddha said the root of all suffering is attachment. In this meditation, you have an opportunity to embrace the idea that everything is temporary and see the beauty in that.

Imagine a huge ice sculpture. It is an intricate carving of the most beautiful mermaid you have ever seen.

Her face is magnificent, and her hair is incredibly detailed and very fluid. Each strand flows into the next.

Her features are well defined, and as you move around the room, her eyes seem to follow you. You are deeply moved by her beauty.

The air is warm, so the sculpture begins to melt slowly. The mermaid turns to a rich, deep-blue liquid that collects in the silver tray placed beneath the sculpture.

You watch as the ice transforms into water. When the last of the sculpture falls into the tray, you walk over and look at the puddle left behind. When you look into the water, you see the glowing reflection of your face.

You sit down and think about life. You are moved by the transformation of the mermaid. As you sit quietly, you feel the spirit of the sculpture surround you. You are filled with a sense of serenity and peace.

You become aware of the perfection of all of life and lovingly embrace life's temporary nature. The mermaid's beauty will always be with you even though the ice no longer exists. You are grateful you had the opportunity to see her beauty and watch it transform.

In this chapter, you deepened your understanding of choices. You realized how powerful it is to connect with your spirit and listen to that wisdom. Focusing on what you do want rather than what you don't want will set you free.

Chapter 16

Where Do We Go from Here?

Your life is an incredible opportunity. It's a gift, and you can do whatever you want with it. You can savor every moment and experience joy, or you can experience pain and suffering. You can be happy or miserable, and you don't have to change anything externally. Life happens out there, but your experience is totally dependent on what you tell yourself about those external events.

This book gives you lots of ways to change that inner dialogue. I remember early in my process; I was so dedicated to my old stories that I realized I was making myself miserable. The next time you start to complain to a friend or watch the news and judge the events, honestly ask yourself, "What do I want to create?" If you tell your friend a "they done me wrong" story, you reinforce any limiting beliefs you have about being a victim. If you look at world events and think, "the news is nothing but bad news and murders," you create a hostile world for yourself that is very fearful.

When I talk to groups about that, someone invariable says, "but the news is awful." When I watch the news, I see lots of opportunities to send love to people, places, and things. Most days, I see the news as an opportunity to open my heart and love. If you want to be happy, practice seeing events in a way that assists you in creating happiness. If you feel sad, afraid, or angry and you are tired of feeling that way, give yourself permission to see things differently.

Your Life

Your life is a blank canvas, and you are the artist. In front of you are all the colors imaginable. You can use all your favorite colors or smear the canvas with all the colors you hate. It is up to you.

My suggestion is to use the colors you like the most.

The Library

This is a fun meditation that helps you feel what it's like to have an infinite number of possibilities.

> *You walk into a large, stately room with vaulted ceilings. Light gently filters through beautiful stained-glass windows. The shelves fill every nook and cranny and go from floor to ceiling.*
>
> *There are ladders that slide effortlessly along so you can easily look at all the millions of volumes the room contains.*
>
> *As you walk in, an old man with a loving voice comes over and asks you if he can help you find anything. You say you aren't sure, and he suggests you look around and let him know if he can be of service.*
>
> *There are several very comfortable chairs, and you wander around looking at all the titles. They're very different than the books you've seen before. The books speak to you as you walk by. They call you by name and remind you of the limitless possibilities available to you. The bindings of the books sparkle and glow.*
>
> *You sit down in the chair closest to the window and relax. You take a deep breath and allow the peace of the place to fill you.*
>
> *The old man comes over and sits across from you. He smiles and begins to tell you about the library. Not only does it contain all the information you could ever want or need, but as soon as you voice your desire, the books will come to you. All you have to do is think about something, and the books appear.*

You try it, and it works. You mentally wonder about being happy, and numerous books on happiness appear. You think about making more money, and books on finance and a variety of careers are stacked neatly on the table next to you.

When you feel overwhelmed by the thought of reading all those books, the old man reminds you the books can speak to you and tell you whatever it is you most need to know.

He tells you that all you ever have to do is sit down in the chair, relax with a question in mind, and allow the information to come to you. The books are just there to remind you that the answers to all your questions lie within.

If you want others to be happy, practice compassion. If you want to be happy, practice compassion.

—Dalai Lama

Clearing Out Your Heart

When your heart is fully open, your experience of life is totally different than when your heart is closed. It is as different as looking out the window with the curtains open or closed. This meditation shows you how to open your heart fully.

Imagine a beautiful gold faucet with water flowing freely from it into a large wooden bucket. The contrast is quite remarkable.

The water slowly spills over the side of the bucket into the pond below. There are water hyacinths, bright pink water lilies, and a large clump of cattails.

It is early morning, and there is a mist coming off the pond. The sun peeks through the trees, creating long rays of buttery sunshine.

There is magic in the air. You sit on a rock and allow yourself to feel the essence of this place.

The sound of the water, the morning calls of the birds awakening, and the sounds of an early summer day surround you.

You feel all your cares and concerns slipping away. For the moment, everything is perfect in your life and in the world around you.

You breathe in the perfection and breathe out anything unlike that perfection. A ray of sun strikes your chest and fills your heart with so much love it is almost overwhelming.

The sun warms your heart and fills your soul. It melts away any old pains, healing all your emotional wounds, and soothes away any cares. You feel like you could sit there forever.

You close your eyes and imagine the water from the golden faucet cleansing your heart and filling your entire being with peace.

You connect with your divine nature at a profound level. You know yourself for the incredible, wonderful, magical, spiritual being you are.

Mirror of Life

Our thoughts, beliefs, assumptions, attitudes, and agreements are constantly mirrored back to us by life. In this meditation, you can play with this mirror and create greater freedom, happiness, and joy in your life.

You enter an inner sanctuary, a place of great wisdom, sanctity, and love. As you open the door, a gentle breeze embraces you. At a profound level, you feel the reverence people felt as they entered this place. You feel honored to have an opportunity to spend time here and absorb its power, peace, and love.

The entire room is made of ancient stones. The walkway is worn smooth by the countless feet that have gone before you.

You stand in the middle of the room, breathe deeply, and feel the peace, love, power, wisdom, and strength that fills the room.

You smile as you look at the mirror standing gracefully in an alcove at the opposite end of the room. It looks like an ancient, sacred altar, and you approach with reverence and awe.

As you look into the mirror, you are struck by the beauty of its frame. The vines and climbing roses around the edges are encased in gold, yet the scent of roses fills the area.

When you look at yourself in the mirror, you can recognize your eyes, but not much else. Before you stands an incredibly beautiful being of light.

You see yourself as you really are instead of how you've come to think you are. You see nothing but perfection, love, gentleness, power, wisdom, and a profound sense of connection. You realize you are one with everything.

You see your life and the world in the mirror. You see the perfection and love reflected there. You stand, transfixed by the beauty you behold in the mirror. You are grateful and amazed by the beauty that is you.

Your sacred space is where you can find yourself again and again.

—Joseph Campbell, author

Creating Bookends

Set yourself up for success by creating bookends for your day. Choose something you can do every morning and every evening to assist you in focusing on your spiritual path and your decision to improve the quality of your life.

It can be as simple as having a sticky note on your bathroom mirror reminding you to think loving thoughts. There are hundreds of things you could do: yoga, meditation, journaling, reading, going for a walk, praying, or doing a visualization from this book.

Pick a day and have a special date with yourself. Pamper yourself, do something nurturing, or play tourist in your own town. Create a special day for yourself. Do it on a regular basis.

Make a list of things you could do each day, and then make it non-negotiable to do them morning and night. Non-negotiable means there is absolutely no room for negotiating. You don't negotiate when you are going to take your next breath; you just breathe.

Make this act of deepening your commitment to your freedom, happiness, and joy each day as much a part of your day as breathing.

Last Bite, Last Day

Often, the last bite of a luscious dessert has far more flavor than the third or fourth. In this meditation, you get to play with savoring it all.

You're at a large banquet with all your friends. You've just finished a delicious dinner. You were so busy talking to your friends that you didn't really pay much attention to what you were eating.

You are laughing and thoroughly relishing each moment. You have already taken a few bites of dessert before you even realize you are eating it.

So, you stop eating and lovingly look at the plate in front of you. You take it all in; you take a deep breath and smell the luscious dessert sitting in front of you.

You take a small bite and savor it. You swirl it around in your mouth, letting it melt on your tongue, and you swallow it, bit by bit.

You take another small bite and are totally mindful of all the subtle flavors. You take another deep breath and allow yourself to be fully present and focused on savoring your dessert. It is much richer and more filling when you allow yourself to really savor it.

You think about your life and decide to savor every moment of it as well. You take the last bite of your dessert and enjoy it completely.

It certainly tastes much better than all the food you consume mindlessly, and you know the same will be true of your life.

Recipe for Living

With the same ingredients, you can make many different dishes. This meditation assists you in coming up with a recipe for your life that works for you.

You are in the center of a holograph that will bring forth anything you want. You gather up all of your favorite ingredients. There are boxes filled with everything you could want or need.

You slowly begin to unwrap them one by one. It feels like you are surrounded by piles and piles of gifts that only you can unwrap.

Each one reveals a variety of ingredients. You realize you could make anything you could possibly imagine. What a gift!

You mix a little of this and a little of that until you get exactly what you want. As you play with all the ingredients, you begin to see all the possibilities. One of the boxes is totally full of recipes.

There are numerous recipes for joy, stress, happiness, love, pain, vibrant health, loneliness, and a deep sense of connection. Some work for you, and some don't.

You realize you can modify them, so they are perfect just for you. Some contain the same ingredients, but the results are very different depending upon how you combine them. As you play, you realize you can create joy and misery with the very same ingredients.

You are overjoyed by the opportunity to play and create whatever you want and are grateful you have all the ingredients you need.

The Choice Is Yours

Happiness really is a choice. You can be as happy as you make up your mind to be. The more fully I realize that all of life is emotionally neutral, the more easily I'm able to consciously choose how I feel. By changing the thoughts I have I change how I feel.

The more I take responsibility for how I feel, the more expansive my vision of life becomes and the more limitless my choices are.

You are the creator of your experience. Taking full responsibility for all your emotions will set you free.

Life Is But a Dream

Remember this nursery rhyme?

> Row, row, row your boat
> Gently down the stream
> Merrily, merrily, merrily, merrily
> Life is but a dream.

There is some profound wisdom in that short little verse. In this meditation, you have the opportunity to wake up in your dream and realize how freeing that choice can be.

Your dreamscape is rich, alive, and full of life. You wander around in your dream much as you do in your life. You react to the events in your dreams rather than initiating the scenes unfolding before you. As you sit on a park bench watching people walking by, you suddenly realize you are in a dream. You wake up in the dream and begin to re-create your experience. You decide you'd like to fly, so you take off and fly. It feels incredibly freeing.

Next, you decide you'd like to float, so you find yourself floating on a cloud. It is fluffy and extremely comfortable. It is sunny and warm out when you decide you would like to see a meteorite shower. In an instant, you are sitting on a mesa with falling stars everywhere.

You begin to realize how extremely powerful it is being awake in your dreams and wonder what would happen if you woke up in life as well.

You realize life is a lot like a dream. You envision your life being easy, full of laughter and joy. Money grows on trees, and you can have whatever you want and need, whenever you want it. You get in touch with your deepest hopes, dreams, and wishes and allow them to be so.

Life is but a dream, and you can move merrily along.

The Journey

Each of us has our own unique journey. This meditation gives you an opportunity to celebrate yours.

You sit at a great council fire in the middle of the desert. It is the time of the new moon, so the sky is filled with millions of stars. A coyote sings off in the distance. The wood crackles and pops, sending hundreds of sparks into the night sky. The smell of pinion wood fills the air. You look around at the faces of the others shining in the firelight, and you feel so grateful to be part of such a magical gathering. At the head of the circle sits the grandmother, draped in her finest ceremonial robes. The sound of the drums is very comforting.

You lean back and look up at the stars just as a shooting star streaks across the heavens. You feel truly blessed. Grandmother calls to you and motions for you to come and sit by her. You sit down where she indicates and look directly into her eyes. The wisdom and the love you see there are almost overwhelming.

She begins by telling you how proud she is of you and how grateful she is that you had the courage to walk your path with love. She invites you to continue your journey with the knowledge of perfection and remembrance that you are always guided by your spirit if you take the time to listen. She blesses you with her love and says a silent prayer over your head. She stands up and stands behind you.

She lovingly touches your head and your heart and begins to sing. It is an ancient song that touches you to the core of your being. The others in the circle stand and begin to sing as well. They sing your song with love and joy.

Your heart is filled. The Grandmother stands before you with her arms raised high, reaching out toward the heavens. She pulls a feather out of her hair and hands it to you. She puts her hand under your chin, looking deeply into your eyes, and says, "You are loved, and you are love. Let your light shine brightly, and listen to the wisdom that lives in your heart. Walk in love and live in peace. You are perfect just the way you are, and you can choose to remember that perfection and deepen your connection to that love. You are a child of spirit, and I am very proud of you."

In that moment, you realize that you are always at the beginning of your journey and at the end of the journey. And you smile, knowing you are where you are and that where you are is absolutely perfect.

In this chapter, you were given access to the library, a place you can gain incredible wisdom, and you also met the Grandmother, a beacon of wisdom and love. One of the greatest gifts you can give yourself is to create bookends for your day and use them daily.

Resources

If you want to go further in your exploration of meditation, here are some resources. Remember, the only thing you can do "wrong" is to fail to use the resources available to you. Play, experiment, and above all else, allow yourself to enjoy the process.

Books

There are thousands of wonderful books out there. Here are some of my favorites. When I was in the midst of doing my healing, every so often I would feel called to the bookstore, where I would wander around the stacks.

The best way I can describe it is a certain book would call to me. Try some of the books on this list or wander around your local bookstore and let the book you need to read next find you.

Many of these books are what I would call oldies but goodies. Most of the authors have more recent books as well.

Channeled

A Course in Miracles. New Christian Church of Full Endeavor, 2005.

Bartholomew. *I Come As a Brother.* High Mesa Press, 1986.

Bartholomew. *Reflections of an Elder Brother.* High Mesa Press, 1989.

Hicks, Ester. *Ask and It Is Given.* Hay House, 2005.

Rodegast, Pat. *Emmanuel's Book.* Bantam Books, 1985.

———. *Emmanuel's Book II.* Bantam Books, 1989.

———. *Emmanuel's Book III.* Bantam Books, 1994.

Healing

Artress, Lauren. *Walking a Sacred Path: Rediscovering the Labyrinth as a Spiritual Tool.* Riverhead Books, 1995.

Borysenko, Joan. *Fire in the Soul.* Warner Books, 1993.

Brennan, Barbara Ann. *Light Emerging: The Journey of Personal Healing.* Bantam Books, 1993.

Brugh, Joy W. *Joy's Way.* Jeremy P. Tarcher, 1979.

Friel, Linda, and John Friel. *Adult Children.* Health Communications, 1988.

Hay, Louise L. *You Can Heal Your Life.* Hay House, Inc., 1984.

Kloss, Jethro. *Back to Eden.* Back to Eden Books, 1985.

Lewis, Thomas, Fari Amini, and Richard Lannon. *A General Theory of Love*. Vintage, 2001.

Muller, Wayne. *Legacy of the Heart*. Fireside, 1992.

Myss, Caroline. *Anatomy of the Spirit*. Harmony Books, 1996.

Rosen, Sidney. *My Voice Will Go with You*. W. W. Norton, 1991.

Summer Rain, Mary. *Earthway*. Pocket Books, 1990.

Welwood, John. *Love and Awakening*. Harper Collins, 1997.

Inspirational

Coelho, Paulo. *The Alchemist*. Harper Collins, 1993.

Girzone, Joseph F. *Joshua*. Macmillan, 1987.

Hanh, Thich Nhat. *Peace Is Every Step*. Bantam Books, 1991.

———. *Touching Peace*. Parallax Press, 1992.

Kornfield, Jack. *A Path with Heart*. Bantam Books, 1993.

Millman, Dan. *The Laws of Spirit*. H. J. Kramer, 1995.

———. *Way of the Peaceful Warrior*. H. J. Kramer, 1984.

Ruiz, Don Miguel. *The Four Agreements*. Amber-Allen, 1997.

———. *The Voice of Knowledge*. Amber-Allen, 2004.

___. Mastery of Love. Amber-Allen, 2011

Tolle, Eckhart. *Practicing the Power of Now*. New World, 2001.

Walsch, Neale Donald. *Conversations with God, Book I Guidebook: An Uncommon Dialogue*. Hampton Roads Publishing Company, 1997.

Williamson, Marianne. *A Return to Love*. Harper Collins, 1992.

Meditation

Benson, Herbert. *The Relaxation Response*. Harper, 2000.

Gawain, Shakti. *Creative Visualization*. New World, 2002.

Kornfield, Jack. *Meditation for Beginners*. Transworld Publishing. 2005.

Levine, Stephen. *Guided Meditations, Explorations, and Healings*. Anchor, 1991.

Shamanism

Andrews, Lynn V. *Woman at the Edge of Two Worlds.* Harper Collins, 1993.

Eagle Feather, Ken. *A Toltec Path.* Hampton Roads, 1995.

Gregg, Susan. *Dance of Power.* I. M. Publishing, 2005.

———. *The Toltec Way.* St. Martins, 2000.

Sams, Jamie. *The Thirteen Original Clan Mothers.* Harper Collins, 1994. Sanchez, Victor. *The Teachings of Don Carlos.* Bear & Co., 1995.

Sun Bear, Wabun, and Barry Weinstock. *The Path of Power.* Prentice Hall, 1987.

Websites

SusanGregg.com   I have visual and guided meditations on my site. I also offer a newsletter, and free semi-daily quotes to encourage you as you proceed on your path. I love hearing from my readers. Feel free to email me with questions, thoughts, and comments.

acim.org   Here you'll find lots of information on *A Course in Miracles.* Embracing these teachings changed my life in many, many powerful and subtle ways.

dailyom.com   This site offers daily quotes that speak to your heart.

whatthebleep.com   This site offers a wonderful way to empower yourself to create what you want.

Glossary

altered state   Any state of consciousness beyond normal waking consciousness. Altered states are useful in relaxation and in personal transformation.

belief   A habitual way of looking at things that really has nothing to do with the truth or reality.

filter system   A system consisting of your beliefs, assumptions, and agreements that stops you from having a direct experience of reality.

guided meditation   Visualizations you can use to improve the quality of your life.

hypnosis   A relaxed mental state that allows you to easily influence and change your beliefs and thoughts.

imagination   Your ability to see something that isn't physically present.

induction   The beginning of a guided meditation in which you are led through a process that will help you relax and be more receptive to the suggestions in the meditation.

journey   The process of going from one place to another.

limbic brain   The portion of the brain related to emotions.

love   From a Latin word meaning "to please." One of several definitions for love is having an unselfish, loyal, and benevolent concern for the good of another. In real life, love is often not about that.

magic   A belief in the ability to influence a supernatural force or the ability to create an illusion. Magic can be created by a change of perspective.

meditation   A relaxed, focused state of being achieved through hundreds of different techniques.

mindfulness   A state of focused awareness.

neuropeptides   Chemicals produced by the brain.

psychobiologists   Researchers who explore the relationship between the brain, the emotions, and other biological processes.

spirit   The part of our consciousness that exists beyond our mind and gives our body life.

spirituality   The intention to focus on one's own spiritual nature.

stress   A physical response to the way you think about external events.

surrender   The key to freedom and the decision to let go of your limitations and your filter system.

trust   To have belief and confidence in our innate goodness and our ability to choose.

visualizations   Mental images and experiences you create internally.

Index

D

E

I

J

K–L

Y

THE AWAKENED LIFE

Explore more of *The Awakened Life* series,
available at fine booksellers everywhere!

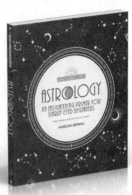

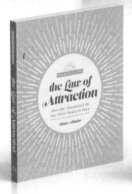